Date Due

THE SACRAMENTO
River of Gold

THE
RIVERS OF AMERICA

Editor
CONSTANCE LINDSAY SKINNER

Assistant Editor   *Art Editor*
ELIZABETH L. GILMAN   RUTH E. ANDERSON

THE SACRAMENTO
River of Gold

by
JULIAN DANA

Illustrated by J. O'H. COSGRAVE II.

FARRAR & RINEHART
INCORPORATED
New York *Toronto*

WAR EDITION

Complete text—reduced size in accordance
with paper conservation orders of the
War Production Board.

TO
THAT NAMELESS FELLOW
THE FIRST MAN
Who Used the River as a Highway

Contents

List of Illustrations

PART ONE

Red Man's River

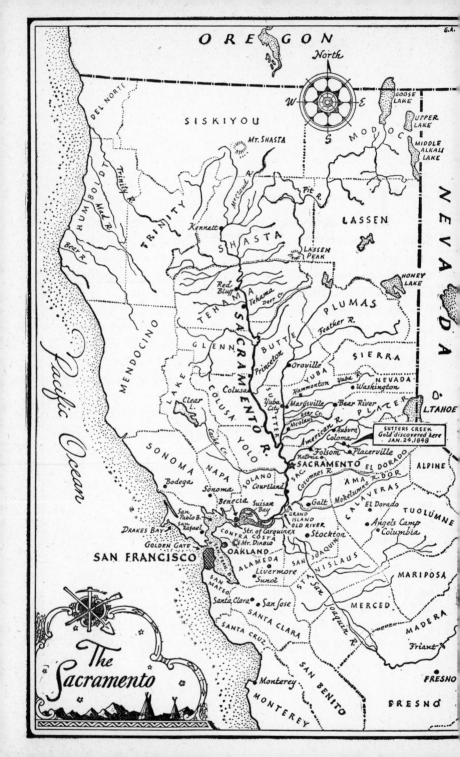

THE Sacramento rises at Big Spring near Mt. Shasta and runs 320 miles to its delta joining with the tidal reaches of the San Joaquin. The river runs south through the Great Valley of California to San Francisco, where it is finally lost in the Golden Gate.

In the beginning it flows through glades where azaleas bloom, past fern and watercress and swaying alders, through mountain meadows to Wagon Wheel Creek, and surges on to meet three tributaries which are born high in marshy meadowlands. The Pit and the McCloud and ten thousand springs and creeks and a dozen lesser rivers run a million miles of white-water way to swell the Sacramento. The torrent whips downward through forests of fir, pine, spruce, and cedar, of madrone, cottonwood, white-petaled dogwood, manzanita, and whitethorn. The rising Shasta Dam interrupts its progress. Soon there will be a lake conserving the waters that will bring life to far-off desert acres.

Below Red Bluff, the Sacramento enters the Great Valley that stretches 400 miles long and half a hundred wide, fenced by an unbroken mountain wall. It courses on past red clay and high boulder banks, past village and rancho and the city that bears the river's name, past factory and houseboat and busy wharf lines, taking on the slowness of a tidal stream where vineyards and orchards grow down to its banks. It wanders through delta lands where colors flame in the growing season like sunrise. Meeting the San Joaquin, it rolls through Suisun and San Pablo bays, through the high-walled Strait of Carquinez and the Bay of St. Francis, past the City No Man Forgets, and through the open gate that fronts the Pacific.

The story of the river begins, vaguely, when a savage Indian empire ruled the Great Valley. But, by sea and trail, white men came to win the river: explorers, soldiers and priests, adventurers, traders and trappers. They were Spaniards, Russians, Americans, Englishmen, and Frenchmen. Nations greedy for lands and treasure sent them. The Spaniards stayed, swept the Red Empire aside, and set up missions in the wilderness. The Russians tried fur gathering and farming. Spain lost the valley to Mexico. The Russians sailed back to Sitka. Then, suddenly, came American dominion and the age of gold. With the gold came wheat, and a new state was born.

Gold and the machine fought against the enduring land. Farmers fought against the "Little Giants" of the hydraulics; against the railroads; against the river in floodtime. Landowners and squatters warred for years over clouded titles. Idealists dreamed of irrigation ditches and did something about it. The history of the Sacramento is the story of the land and its fertility. The people who came to the Great Valley took root in the land, grew with it, and adapted themselves to the changes brought by time.

Legend says that the first white comers to the Sacramento were two valiants of Cortez's band who saw the river in 1520. More than a half century later,

Francis Drake careened the *Golden Hind* in Drakes
Bay. It is certain that he marched inland although
there is no surety he ever reached the river. With
Chaplain Fletcher, he and his expedition held the first
Christian service in 1579 in this Pacific region not far
from the Sacramento's banks.

Real exploration of the stream came two centuries
later. Padres Juan Crespi and Narciso Durán stand beside Pedro Font and Ramon Abella with those who first
went up the river in boats and explored its banks. In
the forerank of the soldiers marched Pedro Fages and
Gabriel Moraga, Captain Luis Argüello, José Joaquin
Moraga and Sergeant José Antonio Sánchez. Later, with
the adventurers came John Sutter of New Helvetia and
Otto von Kotzebue of the Imperial Russian Navy,
Captain Sir Edward Belcher of the Royal Navy, and
Captain W. D. Phelps of Boston. Leading the overland
explorers from the east were Peter Skene Ogden, Jedediah Strong Smith, and Ewing Young. Commanding
the first exploring party of the United States came
Charles Wilkes and Cadwalader Ringgold and George
Emmons. All these save the padres were eager for a
slice of empire, a pile of furs, or both.

They came before gold had sent its fever into the
world, before steamboats plied a river that had known
only tule rafts, dugouts, launches, and whaleboats. Gold
built an exuberant town beside the Golden Gate.
Billions of dollars were carried on the river or brought
overland from the valley foothills.

Gold brought the theater to the river. It was an
inland road for great actors of the East who came barn-
storming through the West: Edwin Booth and "Genial
John" McCullough and Lawrence Barrett and Charles

Kean and Ole Bull and droll Josh Silsbee and a notable score more. Kate Hayes, Adelaide Neilson, Emilie Melville, Laura Keene, Helena Modjeska and Adah Isaacs Menken worked the shining highway. Lola Montez brought a flutter of gilded naughtiness to the river. Lotta Crabtree made it her particular domain. Mark Twain, Bret Harte, Joaquin Miller knew the river, as in a later day did Bayard Taylor, Dion Boucicault, and Ambrose Bierce. Charles C. Nahl, Thomas Hill, William Keith, and even Toby Rosenthal recorded it with paints on canvas.

Here men traveled a thousand trails to private fortune and almost casually marked the trails of progress. They built schools and founded universities, laid steel tracks, put up poles and strung wire. They built churches and laid the devil by the heels and pounded his pitchfork into plowshares—periodically.

The valley had an effect on everyone who came to it. The Yankee, the Frenchman, the Swede, the Dane, the Italian, the Slav, the Irishman, the German, and the Englishman forgot the cramped horizons of their early life. The gold seekers had sons who loved the land. Caution was left behind with another life; here a man could always manage a salute for a dangerous chance. There was a strong rhythm of life in it all—an American rhythm.

2

In 1908 a party of surveyors were at work on Deer Creek, in the southern part of Tehama County, east of the Sacramento River. They were carrying transits and other gear over the ancient hunting grounds of the Yahi, once a mighty tribe ruling the country about

Deer Creek and Mill Creek, not far from Oroville. Making their way through the forbidding region up the rugged watercourse they suddenly came upon a scene from the past. On a huge boulder at the creek edge stood the naked, bronzed figure of a man, a primitive double-pronged fish spear raised high for the kill. His eyes moved from the stream. He whirled like a panther, waved his slim shaft, vanished like a copper shadow.

That night the surveyors had a story to tell in camp. Their answer was a sneer from the cook, who knew the region. Not a wild Indian left in the district, he said. All had been killed off or sent to reservations miles away.

But the next day, as members of the party were crashing a path through tangled brush and scrub oak, an arrow darted out of the bright sky! It shattered against a rock, a foot from the head of an advancing surveyor who dropped a delicate piece of apparatus in his fright.

A council of war was held. The arrow was gingerly examined. It was a stone-tipped shaft, an arrow of the kind used by the Indians a century before. Here, only a few miles from the Sacramento, someone had attacked them with a Stone Age weapon. The surveyors were more puzzled than startled. They moved on, after some delay, but they went with caution and a fast pulse.

Unexpectedly they came upon a camp, concealed in the pepperwood and scrub oak. There was no sign of the warrior with the spear but an old man was crawling away through the underbrush and a middle-aged woman was desperately pushing on his bare rear to hurry his escape. The surveyors let them go. Then under a pile of rabbitskin blankets they found an infirm old woman paralyzed by fright. She made little gurgling noises and pointed to her mouth. They gave her some water and propped her upright.

With the fine zeal of seekers after unique things they despoiled the camp, taking all the bows and arrows, blankets, and other articles in sight. They went back to their tents in triumph. Next day some slight twinge of conscience assailed the band and they returned to offer some presents in exchange for the things they had stolen.

But the campsite was deserted. The old woman, with her rabbitskin mound, and the others had vanished. Anthropologists of the University of California heard the tale some weeks later and rushed to the section to find the fugitives. Their search was vain. Weeks went by. If they still lived, the four had fled without weapons or food into some secret hiding place.

Three years later, on an August morning, a hot dawn broke over Oroville. On the outskirts of the town, in the corral of a slaughterhouse, yapping shepherd dogs shattered the peace of the morning. A butcher rubbed the sleep out of his eyes and lurched upright to look out a dingy window fronting on the corral. As his eyes widened he summoned his companions with a great bellow.

Below, hemmed in by the circle of barking dogs, a man crouched in the mud of the corral. The first sunrays showed him clearly. His hair was burned black close to his head and he wore only a torn piece of rabbitskin clutched around his thin shoulders. His cheeks were sunken and his eyes were hungry and desperate. He had no weapon and he cried out at the dogs shrilly.

The dogs were called off but the men could make nothing of the stranger. He couldn't answer the simplest questions and his words were gibberish. As a last resort the butchers called the sheriff of Butte County by telephone and told him that they had a wild man on their hands and would he please do something about it. The sheriff who arrived was as uncertain as the butchers. He finally decided the coppery-brown stranger wasn't dangerous. After all, he was ready to drop from exhaustion, terror, and hunger. The sheriff put handcuffs on him, draped a stained butcher's apron over his shoulders, and led him away to a jail cell.

Persistent effort was made to learn the man's identity, but nobody knew anything about him. He could hardly be called insane. Obviously he was an Indian. Every man in Oroville who knew any Indian dialect tried it out on the unknown—to no purpose. No word aroused interest in the prisoner. Even offers of food met with no response. He merely sat and watched every movement of his captors with burning, questioning eyes.

The newspapers became interested and the "Wild Man of Oroville" was headlined and featured by the leading California dailies. The late Dr. T. T. Waterman of the University of California Department of Anthropology chanced on a clipping of the story. "I'll bet my hat he's a Yahi!" cried Waterman. Whereupon he rummaged in the file on California Indian languages for a long list of words, packed his bag, and caught the next train. In no time at all Dr. Waterman was in the jail, armed with his list, the sheriff's benediction, and a hunch.

He tried every word in his list with no result. The

prisoner stared blankly into space. At last, desperately, Waterman pointed to the wooden frame of the cot on which the man was sitting and pronounced a strange word as best he could—"si-win-i"—meaning yellow pine. The prisoner's face lost its hunted, hopeless look in a flash. He smiled! With a mounting excitement he pointed to the cot frame. Over and over again with an obvious delight he repeated "si-win-i."

Within a few minutes Dr. Waterman had read an answer out of the riddle of the stranger. The prisoner was a Yahi Indian whose name was Ishi, which means simply "I am a man."

The elated Waterman was sure that Ishi was the warrior with the fishing spear whom the surveyors had seen three years before. Doubtless his companions were dead. Here, in a butcher's apron, sat the last man on earth who knew the language and customs of the Yahi Indians. They had long since been wiped out by the white wave of conquest. Yet, miraculously, a Stone Age man had returned to visit the twentieth century.

Swift arrangements were made for Ishi's release. He was given a bath and new clothes and his appetite became as astonishing as his person. He had found a friend in Dr. Waterman and the world did not seem so hostile a place. The last of the Yahi stepped from the slaughterhouse, where hunger had driven him, to a lifetime haven of security at the University of California.

All his life he had lived within a few miles of a disturbing world, but he knew nothing of its ways. The world had been against him. He had never seen a train at close range until Dr. Waterman led him by the hand to the Oroville station. He had seen trains at a distance and the black smoke they left behind. He had heard the thunder of their wheels, but he did not know that they ran on tracks. To him they were monsters who chased the unwary over the countryside. When the train for San Francisco arrived he whimpered and tried to hide behind his new friend who knew the Yahi word for yellow pine.

A room was fitted up for him at the Museum of Anthropology. It was never otherwise than neat and in perfect order. The regents of the university appointed him a lifetime assistant janitor at the museum with a salary of $25 a month. The hair that he had burned close to his head in sign of mourning for his mother and sister and father grew again and he accepted the white man's clothes, although he detested shoes.

He even learned English after a fashion and his vocabulary of several hundred words served him well. Some of his English was not of the purest. He picked up most of his slang from children who used to visit the museum. I was one of those curious boys who were fascinated by Ishi and his aura of mystery. He had a slight cough that you grew used to. I remember his genial "Sure Mike!" and his patient smile when he did not understand a question. He was a pleasant human shadow, eager to please, often puzzled by the unexplained laughter of ill-bred people.

Ishi's reactions to his new world were unpredictable. Scenes that had been thought certain to amaze him left him without wonder. The high buildings of San Francisco and Oakland were not so high as his native crags, he explained. He was not surprised by electric lights. They were just so much white man's magic. But he was intensely moved by the number of people who passed him on Market Street. In his entire

MT. SHASTA

existence he had never seen more than twenty people together at one time. Now a countless host paraded as far as his eyes could reach. It was a miracle and he could hardly be coaxed away from the sight. A common match was a delight and he kept a box of them near him every moment. He had labored hours to make a fire in his old world. He could understand the beauty and utility of this tiny sliver of wood that called up the gods of flame in a breathless instant.

Automobiles and streetcars were just so much added magic, beyond his comprehension and of trifling interest. But a gleaming metal faucet that spouted clear water when a knob was turned—there was a marvel for a Yahi to gaze at! If a mechanical contrivance came within the range of his earlier experience he was intrigued beyond words. If not, he was simply not interested.

Ishi's first meeting with a window shade was one of moment. He tried to push it aside. It wouldn't push. He tried tentatively to lift it up and it fell back again. Dr. Waterman showed him how to give it a slight jerk and let it roll itself up. An hour later he was still intent on the mystery of where the shade had gone.

But he was forever a fellow of unexpected accomplishments. His life had been primitive. Yet he had a natural kindliness, dignity, and a sense of propriety that no emergency could turn aside. He was very observant of small details and he showed an almost uncanny aptitude for doing everything the way other·people did. The shining table service of his first dinner presented no problems: he used each fork and spoon and knife at the correct intervals merely by watching his companions.

One day he was taken out to see Harry Fowler make his first attempt at a transcontinental flight.

Ishi looked up. "White man up there?" he asked.

He pondered the answer. Then he laughed in his quiet, guttural way and shook his head. That shake was a gentle intimation that white men made life a complicated and puzzling business indeed.

From Ishi came all we know of the language and culture of his people. Some things he would not talk about: the last few years of horror on Deer Creek and the death of those he loved. But he was always glad to talk of the customs of his tribe, always willing to demonstrate techniques of making weapons, and the ways in which they were used. The arrowheads and spear points that he chipped are among the finest specimens ever seen.

But he did not live long in his new world. A deadly bacillus had entered his lungs in that old world which was gone forever. All the miracles of civilization could not save him. On March 25, 1916, Ishi died. At that moment passed the last Stone Age man on the North American continent, the Yahi became an extinct people, and their language became a dead language. But it was not lost, for Ishi saved it from oblivion.

He was buried with all the ceremony of his tribe, as a warrior and a great chief. His bows and arrows lay beside him and bowls of food to stay him until the end of his journey.

3

The "First Californian" died a long, long time ago. He left behind no literature, dead cities, or politician's busts to explain his life and the way he lived it. But he did leave a record of himself for future reference: his bones and his ornaments, his charms and his tools, even his pictographs carved high on granite slopes. These were discovered only recently, by chance. The First Californian might never have taken his place in the record of the human parade if someone had not become intent on making a deep ditch a few miles west of Galt, in the Sacramento Valley. He put a steam shovel to work and dug up the ancient bones.

The graves of the first California race were sunken mounds in the valley. One was found east of Elk Grove near the Cosumnes River, another on the Mokelumne River delta between Walnut Grove and Thornton. Earth had dissolved most of the bones, but a dozen skulls were found in good condition, hidden in alluvial deposits of great antiquity. Above them lay the skeletal remains of another race. The ground between the bones of the two races was of different geologic periods; the first race preceded the second by an incredible number of years.

These early Californians have turned our ideas upside down. Already their later brothers, the scientists, have joined battle over the bones. They have shattered the theory that Indian culture persisted with no change through the centuries. The earlier race differed radically from the later one. The first race used no bow and arrow. It had a grinding slab to prepare food instead of the more modern mortar. The perforated charm-stones represented a different culture. The skulls were thicker and more rugged than those of the race buried above.

Here in the Sacramento Valley lived a heretofore unclassified race type, whom anthropologists now designate as the "First California Man." He has been at rest, the scientists assert, for more than fifteen thousand years with his pitiful treasures grouped about him.

But his bones and trinkets were not all this early inhabitant left behind. On a recent journey into the mountains above the Feather River three Californians came upon hundreds of pictographs carved high on mirror-smooth granite slopes at the head of Rock Creek. These were the records of an extinct people who had perhaps used the section as a great ceremonial gathering place before the Kimshew of the Maidu group came into the Great Valley or roamed the hills. The Kimshew had no tradition that their people made the inscriptions. They knew only a persistent legend that such records existed above their hunting grounds on the south and west branches of the tumbling Feather.

The sun and wind and cold have done their work on the pictographs through the centuries. They are so badly weathered that only the use of lens filters brings out clear and convincing photographs. A few years more and the pictures will be one with the men who made them.

It is not easy to read these records. No man among the remnants of the Kimshew or Concow tribes can decipher more than a few of them. But from the many medicine signs, the lodges enclosing the sun and the stars, and the fact that all point east to the rising sun, our eyes can almost see the tribal hosts climbing to the heights to hold their dances and initiations and shaman-led rites when this Western world was young.

4

In the years when Cortez was fighting Montezuma's warriors and Kit Marlowe and Shakespeare were
writing plays by candlelight and wine, the Indian peo-
ples of the Penutian Empire were unchallenged lords
of the Sacramento and the Great Valley. They had none
of the nomad's curiosity about the new trail just over
the hill. Good hunting and fighting and fishing lured
them only a few miles from their villages and they kept
their tribal borders intact. Invaders were discouraged
by the tall fence of the mountains. The Sierra Nevada
swept along the east and merged with the circlet of the
Tehachapi mountains to the south. Thence the Coast
Range ran as a seawall to the west and met the Sierra
where Shasta, no longer a volcano, stood high in the
north. In this valley, where custom made the land common property of all, lived the great groups of the
Penutian Empire: Maidus, Miwoks, Wintuns, Yokuts
and Costanoans.

No Penutian ever saw the Great Valley as a white
man sees it. He knew the land with the soles of his feet.
His roads were trails and he thought of his valley in
terms of hills and rivers, swamps and meadows, of deer,
acorns, grapes, and wildfowl, of trees, elk, fish, and the
visions of medicine men. He lived with the hills and
the solid plains and he changed his way of life with the
seasons.

There are more native languages credited to Cali-
fornia than to any other equal area in the world: fifty
Indian dialects were spoken in the Sacramento Valley.
A man had but to travel a short distance from his village

to hear a tongue containing only a few words he could understand.

The Wintun lived mostly on a long, fat fringe on the northwestern side of the valley, from the Sacramento River to the Coast Range crest. From the mouth of the Feather to the mouth of Pit River the Wintun rancherias lapped a few miles over the eastern bank of the Sacramento. Where the valley widened to the south they held the tule marshes bordering the river. At the end of the marshes Maidu territory began. The Maidu ruled the country east to the Sierra through which the Feather and American ran, the homeland of Ishi's people, for the Yahi were Yana Maidus. To the south of the Maidu villages, Miwok huts were built along the winding arms of the Sacramento-San Joaquin Delta, and dotted the long westward slope of the Sierra. The Yokuts were masters of every foot of the rich San Joaquin Valley. Close to the Golden Gate, the Costanoans had spread along the coast line, crowded the Hokan away from the outlet, pushed the Pomos to one side and their kinsmen, the listless Esselen, to the other. In the north only the Wintun had pushed beyond the valley barriers. They made the Trinity a Wintun stream and sent a small band to build rancherias on Mad River.

All the valley people were traders. Money—beads and shells—was handled on strings, and counted in tens. It bought salmon, salt, and nuts of the Digger pine that grows at moderate elevations. Farther inland among the hunters it bought bows and arrows, deerskins, and sugar-pine nuts. Wild tobacco from the Honey Lake district was hawked in fragrant bundles to all the tribes.

The men liked games of chance and local wars and dancing. But food came first. Lone Maidu huntsmen wore deer-head masks to stalk their quarry. Occasionally entire villages turned out for a deer or elk hunt with javelins and bows and arrows. Resourceful hunters sometimes separated three or four animals from the herds and followed them in shifts until, without food or rest, they proved easy prey. Bear hunts were ceremonial affairs with many hunters at the kill. Nooses set in coverts caught scurrying rabbits. The ingenious Wintun of the river even used duck decoys of bound rush stems surmounted with stuffed duck heads to lure wildfowl to their nets.

At the headwaters of the Sacramento near Mt. Shasta, the Okwanuchu and Wintun built wooden scaffolds over the swift stream and stood patiently waiting with slender eighteen-foot harpoons to spear the uprushing salmon. On the scaffold the fishermen kept dip-nets for the smaller trout. Seines were used on the lower river. Sometimes soaproot was thrown into the water to poison the fish and bring them senseless to the surface. The Maidu, too, used boats in netting lamprey eel and salmon and trout—tule balsas, log rafts, and flat square-ended dugout canoes. Their more slothful neighbors, the Costanoans of the coast, never bestirred themselves beyond the making of unstable tule rafts, makeshifts that often tossed their owners into rough bay waters.

War weapons were arrows, spears, and clubs. There were no shields. The hill Maidu used to come dancing down to the nearest valley village with which they had a quarrel, clad in waistcoats of mountain mahogany rods, heads bobbing turtle-fashion behind the waistcoat collars. The plains Maidu met them, armored in tough elkhide, dancing also to disconcert the archers, with only the narrow side of their bodies fronting the enemy. The archers were accurate at fifty yards and many of the hill tribes were expert with the slingshot. Prisoners were given the choice of dying by fire or spear.

These valley wars were really only local feuds. Villages never united as allies to fight other villages. Each community felt an instinctive distrust of its neighbors, and consequently there were no elaborate plans of conquest.

Games in the valley had surprising variety and were taken seriously. There were foot races with forfeits of wildfowl and venison, guessing games in which a gambler could lose the deerskin off his back and the wife out of his brush castle. Ball games of different kinds were played with rough wooden spheres. The Costanoans held marathon races. Two contestants sometimes ran as far as a hundred miles kicking a wooden football before them with the flat of their feet, never touching it with their hands. This football marathon was a risky business for the runner. The loser was often roasted by enraged friends who had wagered too highly on his prowess.

There were dances for war, hunting, and courtship. The tribes also danced to amuse themselves and to please the wily shaman. Their musical instruments were flutes of elder, musical bows plucked with the fingers, and Atticus cocoons stuffed with gravel. The medicine men, or shamans, had their good spirits in the sun, stars, and clouds, their evil spirits in dogs, coyotes, and wolves. Among them were the more imaginative leaders in mystic mummery, werebear shamans whose business was to loose dark powers on those who displeased them.

Tempered by tribal fancy, shelter depended on what materials came to hand. The dwellers of the Wintun hill country liked conical, thatched, bark houses. The plains Maidu lived in brush lean-tos and earth-covered sweathouses, all facing riverward. Every ailment was treated for long hours by the shaman in the heated confines of the sweathouses. Each valley village had one dance house and one sweathouse, one house for unmarried girls and another for unmarried men. Living houses quartered a half dozen families, with no partitions and no privacy.

Penutian clothing was scant. Men wore deer or puma skins, tanned side out, a rabbitskin blanket, or a pair of skins sewed together as a mantle. Women wore two maple-bark aprons, front and rear. A wealth of tattoo designs and ear ornaments completed the attire of the socially elect.

A valley suitor followed a simple program. He stayed at home while an able representative approached the girl's father with shell money and soft words. The offering was displayed and discussed. Usually it was returned to indicate that the price was insufficient. Sometimes it was accepted, passed on by a shrewd father to a son, and a similar sum demanded for himself. Often he got it, since the suitor knew a thing or two about halving an offer before sending it out.

Season and place determined what food was eaten. The river people had fish and venison and elk steaks nearly the year round. They had grapes in the harvest months and the Wintun pounded and sifted manzanita berries before cooking them; even used them to make a sweet cider. Young clover was eaten raw. There was a taboo on dog flesh and coyote and wolf. The Pomos ate no grizzly meat. But the Yokuts ate bear steaks with gusto. Grasshoppers, crickets, locusts, and fresh-water clams delighted the Penutian palate. The entire Costanoan shore line is still lined with shell mounds, discarded evidence of a trillion meals of mussels. A dead whale that had washed ashore was also a great event for the Indian gourmets.

Like most Californians who inhabited timberlands, the Maidu burned the country over annually, but he did not burn the forests. A white man's forest fires are a thousandfold more destructive than the fast-running, quick-dying flames of the Maidu. We leave a thick underbrush in our forests that burns long enough to turn our larger trees into $5,000 candles. The Indian never did that. Not that he was protecting the lumber stand. He was interested only in the open country. He proved it by also firing the tule stretches and unwooded lands. It made travel easier, the view better, enemy am-buscades more difficult, hunting simpler. Besides, a crop of herbs and grasses was more to be prized than dry brush.

This was the Red Empire of the valley before invasion. The Penutians were not the most skillful crafts-men among the American Indians, but the Pomos of that family fashioned the best basketry on the North American continent. The valley did not force them to a fierce struggle for survival and it made some tribes languorous and somnolent. The California Indian has not given civilization the herbs and food marvels that are the gifts of his cousins of the Andes and Mexico. Nor do the handful of survivors today give us artists of sensitivity like that delightful Taos girl, Pop-Chalee, or the Navaho, Gerald Nailor, or the Apache, Allan

Houser. These three paint the animals of their native regions with a friendliness, charm, and character equaled only by Walt Disney among the whites. There is no Great Valley Indian to match their decorative, brilliantly colored art.

These men of a savage empire passed without leaving a major legacy to mankind. Their villages are gone and their few survivors live within reservations set up by the white man. Some litter left after their passing has been gathered in museums and hung on collectors' walls. Only the most meager records of their customs and lives and doings are set down in print or manuscript. Incomplete word-lists of their dialects lie shelved in university files, with some of their songs. Pass through the Great Valley today and your eyes will not find any signs of the Red Empire that once existed along the banks of the Sacramento.

PART TWO

Conquest

I

M ANY men sailed the Pacific in cockleshells on imperial business before white exploration of California led finally to American conquest. Juan Rodriguez Cabrillo and his Levantine pilot, Bartolomé Ferrelo, first touched the coast at San Diego in 1542. Drake's piratical voyaging in which he visited Drakes Bay in 1579 had brought a harsh awakening to a Spanish king who had regarded New Spain—Mexico—and his far-flung colonial possessions on the Pacific as secure in their isolation. Cavendish and Hawkins followed Drake in freebooting raids, presaging more frequent attacks on Spain's Pacific colonies, and made some plan of defense by the Spanish crown necessary. The unknown northern coasts of California were especially vulnerable.

Somewhere on the California coast the Straits of Anián were believed to enter the South Sea. Spain was sure Drake had found the straits. If so, what was to prevent English raiders from using this new and easier seaway to Spanish lands and of planting colonies of their own? Whoever held this coast would win the mines of central and northern Mexico, whose tribute was already proving New Spain the richest of Spain's possessions.

In 1584 Francisco de Gali, "the best-trained man

in Mexico in navigation," sailed down the California coast in the Manila galleon—the yearly treasure and trading ship from the Philippines to Acapulco in New Spain—and made a report to the viceroy that stirred added interest in the region. Pedro de Unamuno touched near San Luis Obispo in 1587, three Franciscan friars aboard his small frigate. A mass was said on a hilltop and the land claimed for Spain.

Sebastian Rodriguez Cermeño was sent in 1595 to make a careful survey of the California sea line. His galleon, the *San Agustin*, anchored first at Eureka, was later wrecked in Drakes Bay. He and his company built a boat with a hull hollowed out of a tree trunk, put up a small tattered sail, and went south. They discovered Monterey Bay and completed a 1,500-mile voyage in an open boat along a dangerous coast to Navidad in 1596.

Sebastian Vizcaíno commanded New Spain's next expedition to California. His fleet of two small ships and a frigate reached San Diego in 1602 and ventured on past Cape Mendocino and Cape Blanco, heading into heavy storms. Separated from each other, the boats returned to Acapulco, one crew with the report that it had found a "very great bay" and a "very, very great river" on the voyage.

Vizcaíno's venture marked the end of Spanish exploration in California for a century and a half, the region remaining isolated from 1603 to 1769. A variety of reasons caused Spain's apathy toward further exploration: the death of Philip II; a lack of money to speed colonial expansion; and a realignment in international affairs that lessened the fear of aggression by rival nations in the Pacific.

The energetic statesmanship of Charles III freshened interest in the area when he came to the throne
in 1759. He sent José de Gálvez to New Spain in 1765
as inspector general with instructions to colonize California. Charles III saw this move as imperative. In 1763,
at the close of the Seven Years' War, England had

acquired French possessions east of the Mississippi and
in Canada. This was a menace to Spain's colonial empire
in North America. And a Russian advance from the
Alaskan settlements was possible. The Russians might
even attempt to colonize Vizcaíno's "good port of
Monterey."

The zeal of a few Franciscan friars was to be of
great aid to Spanish crown plans. After Cortez's discovery of the barren reaches of Lower California, the

Jesuits had been given authority to establish missions as permanent settlements in the territory. They had founded fourteen by 1767 and on the mainland, across the gulf from Lower California, which includes what is now northern Sonora and southern Arizona, they had built another line of missions which nearly paralleled those on the peninsula. The names of Ugarte, Salvatierra, and Kino headed the list of these great missionary frontiersmen. These three were dead when, in 1767, Charles III issued a sweeping decree against the Jesuits in his entire kingdom. The Franciscans took over the peninsula missions. Leading the fourteen members of his order who carried on the work of the Jesuits was Fray Junípero Serra. With Francisco Palóu, Juan Crespi, Fermin Francisco Lasuén, and others of his brotherhood, Serra devoted himself to a spiritual conquering of California.

The Franciscans were eager to move north into the new land. Their sovereign, Charles III, demanded at least one port in the unknown reaches of California. Gálvez, in New Spain, was busy in an effort to fulfill the crown's hopes. Uncertainty as to English and Russian plans was a strong spur to action. These pressures led to the founding of twenty-one missions reaching ever northward in California and the claiming of the land for Spain by actual occupation.

The missions were footholds in the region, set at intervals along the unmapped coast. The padres rested a breathing space at each before pushing on to found another haven. With them came a few soldiers as protectors, who also helped the priests fix sun-hardened adobes into walls at mission sites. The natives who accepted the doctrinas of faith were accepted as "neo-

phytes"; the Indians beyond the padres' sphere of influence were "gentiles." A succession of Spanish governors
were appointed who built presidios—walled villages that
served as both fortress and home—as military posts at
San Diego, Santa Barbara, Monterey, and San Francisco. Don Pedro Fages was one of the foremost of these
soldier-governors. Settlers to the region were poor folk
from New Spain, mostly of mixed Aztec and African
blood. Gaspar de Portolá, that gallant leader of the first
expedition to colonize California with settlers from
New Spain, remained only long enough to locate his
charges at strategic places. Then he left, never to return. Juan Bautista de Anza, supposedly the most striking figure of this Spanish period, led the first band of
settlers to reach San Francisco. He selected the site for
the settlement, explored the near-by territory swiftly,
and rode away forever. Captain Luis Antonio Argüello,
another soldier, was the first white man to follow the
Sacramento beyond the point where it meets the San
Joaquin.

Portolá brought a small herd of cattle to the region
with him in 1769. It was the nucleus which, with later
additions and the animals left alive when Anza crossed
the mountains in the deep winter of 1775-1776, formed
the herds of the only great industry in Alta California
during the Spanish-Mexican period.

In 1821 Mexico ceased to be a part of colonial Spain
and in three more years it became a republic. California
acknowledged Mexican rule without incident. The missions had grown rich and powerful, controlling vast
herds and vineyards and groups of neophytes. Secularization—the taking over of the mission properties and
herds by civil government on the pretext of distributing

farming implements and small patches of ground outright to the Indians—came with the republic's birth.
This spoliation, in the course of which many politically
appointed, cattle-raising Mexican settlers took a hand
as self-seeking comisionados, made an end of mission
domination. Political machinery was confused in the
new Mexican dependency: feuds, revolts, and chicanery
were persistent—partly because the Spaniards and the
Mexicans in California distrusted each other.

The French scientist-navigator, La Pérouse, visited
California in 1785; the Englishman George Vancouver,
in 1792; and the Russian Count Rezanof, in 1806.
Trade with Lima began in 1813 when the *Flora* and
Eagle brought cloth to exchange for hides, tallow, grain,
and mission products made by Indian hands. American
and English ships, chiefly otter hunters and whalers, had
begun to barter with the Californios. The *Chatham* had
touched at Monterey in 1794, the first of the tall Boston
ships to make port in California. By 1830 the Yankee
ships were coming in scores and twenty years of gainful
trade lay before them. The period of greatest prosperity
for the ranchos ran from 1828 to the year of American
conquest, 1846.

American official opinion on California had crys-
tallized into action. Manifest Destiny was in the air.
American territory must stretch from sea to sea. The
annexation of Texas and the Mexican War merely
quickened the tempo of the march. The trappers, the
American trading ships, and the settlers crossing the
plains made conquest inevitable. They were helped by
the Wilkes Expedition sent out from the United States
—the first party of white men to explore the Sacramento River from its source to the Pacific.

Neither England, France, nor Russia was behind-hand with expeditions "preliminary to conquest." Otto von Kotzebue, post captain of the Imperial Russian Navy, was Russia's most talented gentleman-about-California. He reached there first in 1816, returning again in 1824, making inland journeys with "scientific eyes" beyond the holdings of Fort Ross, established by the Russians in 1812. Sir Edward Belcher in H.M.S. *Sulphur* made England's empire-survey bid on the Sacramento River in 1837. De Mofras, the Frenchman, followed him, even visiting the Swiss adventurer, John Sutter, in his famous fortress in the Great Valley.

But the United States, which made a fetish of Manifest Destiny, struck too swiftly for the others.

2

In the year 1519 Hernando Cortez conquered Mexico. He had less than a dozen ships, a handful of hard-bitten followers, and a human quality called persistence. He was interested only in finding or taking gold and he died without knowing that his freebooters added a legend of exploration to the story of California.

Before the flag of Spain flew over Mexico City in 1521, two soldiers deserted from Cortez's ranks and fled toward California. They had heard tales about that fabulous place. Since they had accumulated many wounds and very little of Montezuma's treasure in Mexico, they probably felt that California was worth investigating. Spain was at the height of her power and Spanish men-at-arms felt themselves unconquerable. This was still a decade before Pizarro despoiled Peru in Spain's noonday and almost sixty years before Lord

Howard and the wild waves made a sorry show of the Great Armada.

Over desert and plain and river and mountain the two soldiers came, dreaming perhaps of adventure and romance and certainly of gold. To this day old-timers of the Butte County region, with little respect for historians, claim bitterly that these two wanderers were the first white men to gaze upon the Sacramento River and the Great Valley of California.

Weary, hungry, and trail-battered, with one of them near death, the travelers paused one noon on the tributary of what was to them a nameless river. Laboriously they set down on a crumpled rectangle of manuscript a brief record of their passage, terse and undramatic, lacking even a date line—they were not sure how long their journey had taken. They wrapped the rolled manuscript in coils of bark and sealed it deep in the knothole of a great oak. From beneath its shade these two passed into oblivion, hobbling on to find a grave somewhere without a marker.

More than three centuries and a half later—in April, 1879—two miners, slashing down an old oak on the Middle Fork of the Feather River, came upon a cracked, almost illegible manuscript set in the middle of the tree. From the outer bark, the tree appeared whole and sound. Not knowing Spanish, the tree-choppers were only mildly interested in their find. Indeed, little mention was made of the incident until by chance, ten years later, the manuscript was translated by a Spanish scholar who immediately began to run a temperature. For final proof it was dispatched to the director of the Museo Naval in Madrid, and was never returned. In the 1932 report of Dr. Julio Fernando Gullen y Tato, director of the Museo Naval, I find no mention of the manuscript. And so the story stands.

Whether an imaginative newspaperman of the seventies needed a filler or whether an authentic record of California's youth has been lost through stupidity is not important. This story, and others like it, create a warm atmosphere around the region and its drama.

3

The first dusty-robed padres who built homes and made converts in California came to give and not to take. Audacious in their faith, they journeyed with thin bodies and feet bruised by the trail. They were sure that the long line of adobe missions stretching behind them would stand forever in the new land.

In 1772 Father Juan Crespi and Don Pedro Fages stood on the northern flanks of Mt. Diablo and looked down on the delta region and the misty silver threads of the Sacramento and the San Joaquin. But they went no farther. Father Pedro Font and Juan Bautista de Anza wandered over the same section four years later, shortly after the founding of the mission at San Francisco. José Joaquin Moraga plodded for three days along the banks of the San Joaquin that same year but did not reach the Sacramento.

Lieutenant Gabriel Moraga made a swift circle through the San Joaquin Valley in 1806, alert for possible mission sites and runaway neophytes who had found doctrinas not to their liking. Not content with this, he led a dozen soldiers from Mission San José on September 25, 1808, on a month's journey, by way of

Sunol and Livermore, to the San Joaquin. Crossing rivers and plain, he named the lower Feather River the Sacramento! A few days later he touched the Upper Sacramento near Stony Creek and called it the *Jesus Maria*, a name it bore for some time.

It was three years after Moraga's trips that the first microscopic boat-invasion of the Sacramento by white men took place. Four launches with sixty-eight people aboard left the Presidio anchorage on San Francisco Bay, October 15, 1811, for a fifteen-day trip into the delta channels and islands. No one knew anything about the country to be visited, not even the coastal neophytes who did the rowing. Padres Abella and Fortini shepherded the party and they were hoping to win new converts in the strange region.

Sergeant José Antonio Sánchez commanded the expedition. The sergeant was a singularly winning fellow whose liking for horse races and all games of chance kept him in spiritual disrepute until his death. Indeed, a padre brooded for some time over Sánchez' body, seeking heavenly guidance as to whether such a sinner could be buried in consecrated ground. It is pleasant to record that the sergeant was finally admitted to the sacrosanct dust. Such a lighthearted human spirit as that of the fun-loving Sánchez, first white man to command a recorded navigation of the Sacramento, surely deserved the best in heaven that his faith could accord him.

It took Sánchez' launches two days to reach Suisun Bay and camp on what is now Brown's Island, where the native Ompines had a fishing station. The expedition passed through what is now Three Mile Slough at the head of Sherman Island into the "northern river of San

Francisco"—the Sacramento. Along the banks they found a few Indians who seemed friendly and curious. Some of the less-nimble aged and sick were baptized by the joyous fathers.

Half a league onward they turned from their short journey on the Sacramento into the right and smaller channel of the San Joaquin—the West Channel—and sailed east and south on a winding course for four days, sleeping on the boats at night and making no landing. On the morning of the fifth day they retraced their way and carried back to the Presidio their meager news of low-lying river lands and a great plain, covered with wild herds, that seemed to stretch endlessly into the distance.

It remained for Captain Luis Antonio Argüello to make the first important land-and-water explorations of the Sacramento River. Argüello was a slim, neat person, with a quick laugh and a ready word. He was popular with his men, reckless and peevish under any restraint, fond of wine and horses and ribald companions and always ready to dance. He was born at the Presidio of San Francisco in 1784 and his father before him was comandante of the Presidio Company. The Argüellos were nobly born, out of the hidalgo strain of Old Spain. Don Luis's two brothers, Santiago and Genacio, served with him as he rose from cadet to alferez, from teniente to captain, and finally to the post of ranking officer.

In 1817 Don Luis took ten soldiers, and ten neophytes as oarsmen, in his launch *San Rafaela* and sailed for the Unknown River. With him, in the launch *San José*, went Padre Presidente Narciso Durán of the mission at San Francisco and Padre Ramon Abella of

Mission San José. Father Durán kept a careful diary from May 13th, the day of departure, until May 26th, the day of safe return. It was ten o'clock of a sunny morning that Comandante Argüello ordered his boats from the Presidio anchorage. At noon they stopped on Angel Island for lunch. Night found them well beyond Point San Pablo, where they made shore by starlight. At dawn of the second day the oarsmen were pulling the blunt-nosed boats against a heavy head wind, their dark bodies wet with sweat and salt spray. In midafternoon "near the Strait of the Chupcanes" the harsh wind whipped itself into a storm.

Don Luis landed on Brown's Island and built a roaring fire. But the padres in the following boat did not arrive until after dark and had passed Argüello's landfall before his fire blazed high. The gale kept the fathers' launch from returning and they rowed on, up the Sacramento River now, and finally landed in the darkness on a small tule island that was covered with water at high tide. Here they spent the night on a spot full of brambles, whipped by a cold wind.

In the stormy dawn, as Argüello worked up the river to meet the padres' boat, his mainmast split. Its pieces pelted down like a hail of knives, the largest one missing Don Luis's head by a foot, yet no one got so much as a scratch. The passengers of the *San Rafaela* were in a grateful mood when they reached the *San José*, although the storm still beat upon them.

On the third morning, a holy day, the boats made six more leagues up the river. Both parties then landed and the "mass was sung." The stream was in flood and the place was unsheltered. They pressed on and at nightfall reached "Lomas de los Ompines, the hills sheltering us from the gale." The *San José* struck a submerged log that evening just before landfall but luckily she rode over the snag without tearing a hole in her hull.

All that night a great wind lashed them. Then, at dawn, it died. With the sun a pleasant warmth went deep into chilled bones. For seven shining days Don Luis and his companions rowed up the river, the banks of which seemed "like a king's park" with their lanes of poplar, cottonwood, alder, and oak. Masses of grape-vines dipped over the banks of the river. They passed numberless tributaries and saw the smoke of Indian rancherias pluming the country inland. But they had little luck in finding villagers who did not vanish as the launches approached. Once they landed for Don Luis to parley with some Indians who decided on peace. At night they tied up to the banks with sentries alert to repel any red attack. They watched the great herds of deer and elk and bands of grizzlies that ranged the Great Valley plain, and then looked toward the Sierra Nevadas and their jagged whiteness far away with a hope "that a pass will one day be discovered."

At midafternoon of May 20th they blazed a cross on an oak to mark the farthest point of their explora-tion. Then Don Luis signaled a return and the swift current swept them downstream fourteen leagues by sunset. Next morning they branched left into a tribu-tary stream of the Sacramento and found an abandoned rancheria of the Ochejamnes. Just before reaching the San Joaquin through the maze of flooded waterways they came upon a village of Guaypems where the padres baptized seven people. It was a happy moment.

On May 22nd Don Luis left the padres' launch and headed for two or three small islands where it was reported that some "fugitive neophytes from Mission San José were living together in hiding." The *San José* went on alone up the San Joaquin—at night now, since the heat of the day was too terrific for the oarsmen.

A day later the padres rejoined an impatient Don Luis near Bradford's Island and the launches began their homeward journey. They were forced to wait for high tide at the mouth of the San Joaquin since the sand bar there blocked passage at low water. As the sun rose, May 26th, having urged the weary rowers on through the last night, they beached at the Presidio anchorage and a mass was said in thankfulness for their safe return.

It was fortunate that the articulate Father Durán wrote about the river journey. If we had depended upon Don Luis for such an account we would have found only a routine report of the orders he executed. He had no taste for heroics in prose. His report consisted of a few terse sentences. It was Don Luis's way of life and this journey measured just so many days of it—a common enough performance in his mind, even if he was making a first passage up an uncharted river.

Three years later Don Luis had another ambition. Not only would be penetrate this time to where the Sacramento began, but he would go as far as the Columbia! As he left the Presidio his launches were crammed with a formidable array of thirty-five mounted men—soldados de cuera—and twenty infantry. The day was October 18, 1821. They landed at Carquinez Strait and crossed the Suisun plains. Keeping a north and easterly course, they reached the western bank of the Sacramento and began their march. It was difficult going. Argüello had purposely delayed the start to miss the midsummer heat but the Indians attacked his land force with a bitterness and persistency that he had not encountered on the boat journey. Arrows rained on the column and the horses dripped blood as they walked. Some of the mounts drank alkali water and died. Others were lamed. Every new rancheria the army passed sent out its quota of attackers. Supplies ran short and with Indians on every hand it was almost impossible to hunt.

Nevertheless, a scrawling map was made. Mountains and creeks were named. Though the map was subsequently lost, it is certain that Don Luis and his troops did not march farther than Mendocino County and their retreat was considerably more rapid than their advance. With but eleven horsemen—the rest had been added to the column of infantry—this first white army to invade the Great Valley and its river came to San Rafael on November 12th and rested three long days before returning to the Presidio across the bay. Regardless of the belief expressed by several modern chroniclers, Don Luis never reached the Columbia.

Nor did he again invade the river region. The sun of Spain set and he became the first executive of the province under the banner of Mexico. The job of governorship, when all men seemed set against change, was a brittle, touchy business. His soldiers went underfed and unpaid. He wrote letters and threatened and cajoled and argued and supplicated. The padres heeded him, more because of personal friendship than from liking for the new authority. They gave him food and cattle and cloth from the mission looms to make uniforms for his troops. After a time matters became less acute. But when Echeandia was named his successor Don Luis was a joyous man. Here was an end of thankless responsibility, of the bitter days of endless squabbling.

The years had put their mark upon him. Doña Rafaela Sal, his first wife, was long dead and he had married Doña Soledad Ortega. "A good match," said his brother Santiago good-humoredly. "It will keep our spendthrift from folly—I hope."

It did. For a time. But wine helped him forget the unfriendliness and the stupidities of people who harass a governor filled with the best intentions. When Don Luis left off being governor and went back to his post as comandante of the Presidio of San Francisco he felt that wine was his best friend. And he made much of the friendship.

The Presidio Company became a place of wassail and fellowship. Strange tales were heard of laxity and unmilitary procedure. Don Luis was removed—"not for cause," Echeandia hastened to assert, moving reluctantly in this case, "but for the good of the service."

His successor, Martínez, as comandante of the Presidio, was none too kind in preparing Don Luis' service record. It read:

> Valor—accredited.
> Capacity—bastante.
> Military Conduct—apatica.
> Civil—drunkard.
> Health—broken.
> Loyalty—supposed faithful.

So Don Luis, denied his military life and many of his old companions, made more of his friendship with the grape. He began to boast that he would go up the river—yes, to its very source!

And then one March day in 1830—it was the

seventh day of the month—Don Luis lay in his bed and received the last sacraments from Father Estenaga. Don Luis admitted he was going on a journey—"up the smiling river to the north," he said. "It is a great river and I have a wish to see the beginning of it—I know it is born in the hills I saw that rise beyond. I ask your blessing in this venture, father." And Padre Estenaga blessed the journey Don Luis was taking and he set out upon it.

He lies buried in the churchyard of the Mission Dolores, beside Doña Rafaela, his first love. In his youth he was a valorous gentleman, a just and kindly one, and at the end he was something of a fool. But he was the first white man who explored the river and marched upon its banks when it was an unknown stream.

4

In the early nineteenth century Russia had ambitious schemes for a Russian California. At the headquarters of the Russian-American Fur Company at Sitka, in Alaska, plans were made to move southward. Kuskof led a party to establish the new post of Fort Ross in 1812, six years after Count Rezanof's visit to San Francisco. With him came officers of the fur company, farmers, and native Kodiaks and Aleuts from the north. These natives were the fur takers whose javelins and seagoing bidarkas, fashioned of sea-otter skins stretched tightly over wooden frames, made it possible for them to scour the coast and Farallones region for rich pelts.

Captain Otto von Kotzebue of the Imperial Russian Navy paid the Russian colony more than a casual call in 1816, and he also visited Spanish San Francisco. He commanded the *Rurik* on a world cruise catalogued officially as a "scientific expedition." It was the habit of the day to label each empire-seeking boatload as an "Around the World Scientific Expedition." No one was fooled by the frayed word-costume. Most of these expeditions forgot their globe-circling aspirations when they happened upon a territory where they could plant a flag.

On that first visit von Kotzebue and his scientific staff contented themselves with journeys about the bay of San Francisco and the surrounding shore. Louis de Chamisso, a French naturalist, was aboard the *Rurik*. As he wandered over the poppy-covered spring hills near San Francisco, he named the California poppy *Eschscholtzia California* after his young friend, Johann Friedrich Eschscholtz, zoologist of the party.

Any inland marches were politely but firmly discouraged by the Spanish authorities. Von Kotzebue was forced to sail away with only vague surmises about the river valley, no clearer than those of the Ross colonists. But he was a man of purpose. His frigate, the *Enterprise,* crept through the swift tides of the Golden Gate in 1824 and this time von Kotzebue was determined to have his own way, regardless of official opposition. Although his social graces appear to have been of the slightest, he finally secured the grudging consent of the comandante of the Presidio for a brief inland excursion. The padres were persuaded to lend him Marco, the neophyte pilot from the mission, who knew the bay well and had acted as the captain's guide on his first visit.

While von Kotzebue was concluding arrangements

at the Presidio and the mission, Dr. Eschscholtz had
gone to Fort Ross by ship's boat to bring back some
twenty Aleuts and their bidarkas. This flotilla promised
to be excellent water cavalry to fend off any river dangers and the captain was delighted at his own foresight
in the matter.

By the time Eschscholtz returned with the fur
hunters von Kotzebue had two small boats waiting,
a barcasse and a shallop, and had even made a few preliminary jaunts about the bay islands. The party left the
Enterprise in a November dawn, a half dozen seamen
at the oars of each boat. The Aleuts rushed about like
sportive seals, their bidarkas weaving antic trails in the
boat wakes as the course led north and east through San
Pablo Bay and Carquinez Strait and into the waters
of Suisun.

No stranger fleet ever went up the river. They
traveled as far as the modern Freeport. Von Kotzebue
was charmed by the "broad, beautiful stream, sometimes winding between high, steep banks, sometimes
gliding through smiling meadows where great herds of
deer were grazing. In every direction the landscape was
a sweep of beauty and luxuriance. Our Aleutians here
straggled about in their little baidars and pursued the
game with which land and water were stocked. They
had never seen it in such plenty and being passionately
fond of the chase they fired without ceasing, even
bringing down some of the game with a javelin. The
Aleutians were as much at home in their little leathern
canoes as our Cossacks on horseback. They follow their
prey with the greatest rapidity in any direction and it
seldom escapes them. White and gray pelicans, twice
the size of our geese, were here in great numbers. An

Aleutian followed a flock of these birds on the river and killed one of them with the javelin. The rest of the birds took this so ill that they attacked the murderer and beat him severely with their beaks and wings before the other baidars could come to his rescue. The frequent appearance of pelicans on the river proves it abounds with fish, which our pilot Marco was quick to affirm. We ourselves saw many great fish leap beyond the surface of the water."

The Russians pitched their tents each night in meadow stretches and Otto von Kotzebue was increasingly enchanted with the country. On the third day, "I climbed a hill on the western bank to enjoy a more extensive prospect. Tree besprinkled hills of moderate heights rose in the west. In the east and southeast were the icy Sierra. Between them and the river the country is low, flat and thickly-wooded, crossed by an infinite number of streams which divide the whole of it into islands. We had not yet met a single native. But the columns of smoke which rose from this abundantly irrigated section showed that they had taken refuge where the dragoons and their lassos could not follow to convert them."

Von Kotzebue enthused over the soil's richness, the shade trees, the clusters of grapes with their sweet, tangy flavor, the possibility of rich wheat harvests. He set down: "The chase furnished us with ample and profitable amusement. An abundance of deer, large and small, ranged the country, and geese, ducks, and cranes covered the river. There was such a superfluity of game that those among us who had never been sportsmen before, when once they took a gun in hand, could not set it down for the sheer joy of it."

The nights appear to have been fairly lively and interesting. "When it grew dark we kindled large fires so that our hunters, some of whom invariably lost their way because of eagerness in the chase, might recover the camp. In the night we were much disturbed by bears, which pursued the deer by starlight quite close to our tents. By one clear moon we plainly saw a stag spring into the river to escape a bear. His enemy, however, jumped in after him, and both swam down the stream until they passed a bend beyond our sight."

The "sportsmen" began their return with some regret. At one point von Kotzebue found a stake driven into the earth with a bunch of feathers dangling from its top as a weathercock. Here and there tule canoes were found, hidden. But no Indians. The valley and river dwellers were wary of all travelers and no doubt the sight of an Aleut with a javelin did little to put a Penutian into a visiting mood.

Nevertheless, an inquisitive polecat strolled into von Kotzebue's tent during the last night on land before the party reached the *Enterprise*. Otto was never at a loss for words to lengthen an issue and he reports that the "insufferable creature has so abominable a smell that I found its vicinity practically insupportable." He also wrote harshly of the "little wolves that ate our venison on that last night." To make the evening more memorable a rattlesnake captured by Dr. Eschscholtz on the river escaped from its basket in one of the tents. After that the entire company kept a jittery watch until dawn.

Without any formal good-byes to the Spanish officials, von Kotzebue sailed for the Sandwich Islands, barely escaping disaster on a rock as the *Enterprise* navigated the Golden Gate without a pilot. His aides, the Aleuts, returned to Ross. What von Kotzebue purposely failed to mention in his record of the river journey was that many sea otters fell prey to the Aleuts in the bay waters. That might have fired his Spanish hosts to action. These hunters and their bidarkas eventually spelled extinction to the sea otter on the California coast. But, in 1939, after the species had been seemingly dead for a century, a small band of some eighty were seen and photographed on the Monterey coast. This tiny group, perhaps sheltered in a hidden water cavern by the rugged sea line, have made their battle against death. Now, for the first time in this century, they have shown themselves and Uncle Sam has already been forced to appoint official guardians of the herd to see that no potshooting hunter bags an otter pelt.

After von Kotzebue, England sent on official investigation of the Sacramento River under Sir Edward Belcher of the Royal Navy in 1837. Shortly afterward France dispatched a one-man goodwill tour in the notably sweet-scented person of M. Eugène Duflot de Mofras. Trappers of the Hudson's Bay and Northwest companies had long preceded Sir Edward to the Sacramento. As early as 1814, Alexander Henry of the Northwest Company wrote in his diary that "Arrangements were made with Caron and Day, freemen, on halves for the Spanish River"—proof that trappers had long since moved south to the Sacramento. But the "Around the World Scientific Expedition" aboard H.M.S. *Sulphur* was the first English group to chart a portion of the stream. De Mofras journeyed up the river and the valley in dapper and more leisurely

fashion. He was a latecomer to a scene where the tides
of history were running swiftly around him. He is not
remembered as a spy of empire, but chiefly as a soft-
pawed social lion and husband baiter, and as the author
of a book of ecstatic improbabilities.

Belcher took two ship's boats "150 miles upstream
to the head of navigation." Full of fine promises and
stuffed with secret orders, Sir Edward, despite his military training, proved as talented a lace-at-the-throat
and hemlock-in-the-cup diplomat as was ever turned
out by an English family born to the business. He made
his river trek with General Mariano Guadalupe Vallejo's
blessing on the assurance that a copy of the chart of his
journey, to be added to the official Mexican files, would
be left with Vallejo on his return. Sir Edward grew
forgetful at the last moment and the *Sulphur* raced
out of the Golden Gate, leaving a chartless Vallejo
seething on the shore and twenty meddlesome English
deserters moving in twenty different directions over the
countryside, a troublesome exchange to the general who
wanted only a map.

5

Spain tried to keep all visitors from her American
colonial borders, a task as futile in California's case as
trying to keep honeybees from clover fields. Adventurers, traders, and hunters swarmed across the long
frontier. And when Mexico inherited California from
Spain in 1821 the intrusions continued.

The northernmost villages of the Spanish colony
had been built as outposts against foreign intruders, but
they served only to attract and concentrate first the
French and later the Anglo-American invaders. The

whole eastern flank of Mexico's slender and vulnerable salient, what is today California, Nevada, Utah, Arizona, and New Mexico, was subject to merciless foreign commercial pressure as early as 1822. These alien adventurers, or "splendid wayfarers" as Niehardt calls them, were naturally restless and never satisfied. It was inevitable that they should reach the Sacramento River and make the conquest of the Great Valley.

Also, the bargain stores under sail from New England were bringing goods to California: ironware and hardware, textiles of every variety, silks and satins, combs and scents and slippers, and honest old Colonial furniture. For these luxuries the ranchero traded his hides at a uniform two dollars each and his tallow at a dollar and a half per arroba of twenty-five pounds. Trade was brisk when the Boston ships anchored at spots from San Diego to San Francisco. The Yankees always put in at Monterey first, to pay duties that ran as high as a hundred per cent. That is, nearly always. There was friendly smuggling and keen competition in the trade. The ranchero's sole articles of barter were his hides and tallow. The matanza, or slaughter, was only an annual affair. California was a land without money, gold or silver or paper. A ranchero's promise to pay was all the surety required by any man.

If competing traders landed on the coast at the same time, there was vigorous rivalry for all the available business. Supercargoes climbed on horses and rode the country making contracts for hides, watching for deserters from the ships, and telling the inland ranchos when the vessel *Don Quixote, Albert, Pilgrim,* or whatever it was, would arrive at the nearest anchorage.

The trading meetings were carnival days. Dancing

and dining, gambling and horse racing, and bear-and-bull fighting were mixed with trading. The californios got along well with the merchant-sailors. A mutual regard grew with the years and the house flags of Bryant-Sturgis and other Boston shipping firms were known and trusted up and down the coast. As ambassadors of goodwill and fair dealing—sharp but fair—the Yankees had no equal.

At the same time American trappers and traders were pushing west, meeting Spanish neighbors as they went. These Americans hoped to find wealth and romance, and often they did. First they met the lady of their dreams in Nacogdoches and then, as they moved farther overland, in San Antonio, in Santa Fé, in Taos, and in Los Angeles. When they came back from the lands where all harvests ripen early, they talked of Spanish girls with dark eyes and black hair who liked Americans. These tales, as much as the hope of fortune, brought more adventurers to the West.

These men wrote a chapter in the expanding history of America as they wandered. Their vanguards liked the Spanish borderlands. And when muscles grew less elastic and joints a trifle stiffer, the Spanish towns were comfortable spots for rovers to forsake the trail, settle down, and become members of old families.

In time these mountaineers in their Indian shoes came to the Sacramento and the Great Valley. The rank and file was made up of brawling adventure lovers with the horizon forever in their hearts and a fondness for a life of half savagery tucked tightly under their coonskin bonnets. They strode through the Mexican lands, more often without permission than with it. They were a tireless, buckskinned, fully armed host who were happy either running keelboats, piling mountains of furs on pack horses, or stealing Mexican mounts. They spent their lives clinching stinking saddle girths, wading waist-deep in swift streams to set beaver traps, stalking grizzly or cougar or Indian, spinning flabbergasting yarns or howling unprintable songs in drunken revels around campfires that never burned twice in the same ashes.

Out of this illiterate legion came the paradox of Jedediah Strong Smith, temperate and intelligent and shrewd, the first American trapper to reach the river. Scaling the high Rockies in the spring of 1825 he and his company trapped near Great Salt Lake for a time. Then he led the way west to the Humboldt and named it Mary's River. Following down that stream he and his men crossed the Sierra Nevada into the Great Valley of California in July.

Even these wanderers were amazed at the wild life about them. Promptly Smith established the headquarters of the Rocky Mountain Fur Company on the American River near the modern Folsom. Then leaving all but two of his men, he recrossed the Sierra through what was later Walker's Pass and hurried on to the rendezvous at Green River to tell the trappers there of the numberless pelts waiting in the great "Spanish Valley." Near Mono Lake, on that return, Smith picked up samples of rich gold ore. This, added to his tales of the fur catch, started a furor of talk and plans.

Next season Smith came back with a dozen companions, taking care to inspect the route for placer gold along the way. This time he trekked as far south as the Mohave villages on the sun-blasted stretches of the Colorado, pressed on across the Mohave Desert to reach

Mission San Gabriel in December of 1826, laden with beaverskins and traps. They created a sensation. Officials shook sober heads. But the señoritas peered through drawn curtains at the tall strangers with friendly eyes.

Mission San Gabriel was a pleasant place to men from ice-covered hills and parched wastelands. Harrison Rogers of the party put down in his diary a benediction on the "dinner of fish and fowl, beans, potatoes—grapes as dessert, wine, gin, and water aplenty" that the kindly padres set before the wayfarers. The Franciscans, though "Catholicks by profession," pleased Mr. Rogers very much. He acknowledged them as "gentlemen of the first class" and they delighted the visiting Presbyterian by allowing him "full liberty of conscience," while he, conscienceless fellow, tried to correct their theology and save their souls!

The head-shaking officials ordered Smith and his party to San Diego where they pleaded their case before the governor. He took away their passports and directed them to leave Mexican soil immediately. Had there not been a few Boston ships in harbor at the time, whose officers made swift intercession for their countrymen, it might have gone hard with the fur poachers.

Promising to leave the territory as soon as possible, Smith rode with his party from San Diego to the southern floor of the Great Valley. In May, 1827, he was in camp near San José and his presence disturbed Padre Narciso Durán. Smith wrote him a letter, allaying his fears and puzzlement by saying that "we are Americans on our way to the River Columbia, having passports to proceed on to that place." He explained, further, that he and his friends found "our situation most unpleasant, being destitute of clothing and most of the necessities of life, wild meat being our principal subsistence." He signed himself: "I am, Reverend Father, your strange but real friend and Christian brother. J. S. Smith."

Finally the expedition pushed overland and joined forces with the fur hunters who had been left at the American River headquarters. With spirits higher and pack horses smothered under fine pelts, the reunited party started for the Columbia. Near the head of the Sacramento Valley they turned west to find the Pacific near the mouth of Russian River. But when Smith and his men ventured up the coast they rode to disaster. At the Umpqua River, near Cape Arago, Indians attacked them in the night. In the darkness only Daniel Prior, Richard Laughlin, and Smith escaped. The rest died among their furs and traps, yelling war cries as savage as those which had awakened them for the last time.

With nothing left but their weapons the weary survivors made Fort Vancouver and reported their misfortunes to the sympathetic Dr. McLaughlin of the Hudson's Bay Company. He had always followed a firm policy of protecting white men "against Indian aggression." He sent an expedition which "chastised the malefactors"—presumably the malefactors, in their turn, died in the night. Most of the pelts and traps were recovered.

Smith had made a pledge to McLaughlin that, if aid was given him, he would guide Hudson's Bay men into the Great Valley of California, the fur storehouse he had just left. Smith kept his promise by proxy. In the late fall of 1827 Daniel Prior, of his party, guided a Hudson's Bay brigade under Alexander Roderick Mc-Leod back to the Sacramento Valley by the luckless trail Smith had made. Winter snows trapped them later on the McCloud River. They lost all their mounts, cached their furs, and finally won their way through to Vancouver. The river bore McLeod's name but a resident who came long after, Ross McCloud, lived there so many years that the mapmakers have incorrectly spelled it McCloud.

After McLeod's return, Jedediah Smith joined a party under Peter Skene Ogden, planning to guide it to the Great Valley by a safer route. The party passed by way of the Columbia and on to the source of Lewis River. There Smith left Ogden. Ogden went southwest through Utah and Nevada. He entered the San Joaquin Valley through Walker's Pass, trapped on the rich, level floor of the Upper Valley, and followed Smith's first footsteps back to Vancouver.

The Great Valley had not been ungenerous to Jedediah Strong Smith. But the side trails had been perilous. Disheartened, he sold his interest in the Rocky Mountain Fur Company the next year. In 1831 a cloud of arrows struck him down in the dry bed of the Cimarron, near Taos. His companions buried him in a shallow grave in a river bed while the rollicking fur brigades of Michel La Framboise were singing far away in the Great Valley.

He was the first of California's overland fur seekers. He never took a fortune from the wilderness, but he led the way. Alexander Roderick McLeod and Peter Skene Ogden and Michel La Framboise and Ewing Young followed him. The tide grew stronger. Joseph Reddeford Walker and more scores of mountaineers found their way to the river valley. Old Sante Fé traders were among them—John Sutter, Benito Wilson,

John Marsh, John C. Yount, J. J. Warner, William Workman, Isaac Graham, and William Wolfskill. John Charles Frémont followed in 1842. When Charles Wilkes and his reports, Thomas Ap Catesby Jones and his frigates, Thomas Oliver Larkin and his diplomacies, and the mapmaking Frémont appeared on the scene, America had already decided that California belonged to her.

6

Johann Augustus Suter, known to Americans as John Sutter, was the first white man to find personal power in the Sacramento Valley. In 1834 this Swiss papermaker and publisher's clerk was thirty-one and success had so far eluded him. Debts had piled high. To see his wife, Anna, and their four children suffering for lack of things he was too poor to buy prodded him to constant schemes.

Rumor had it that in America there was land for the taking. The idea grew in Sutter's mind. A resolve, almost of desperation, came to him. He would go to the United States. He wanted a home free of debts, a chance to begin again.

His brother, Friedrich, pledged himself to care for Johann's family in his absence. Saying good-bye to them all, Sutter promised to send money soon to bring them to their new home. He was always full of promises and always hoped to keep them. On another continent he proved himself a plausible, engaging optimist who could make his listeners see that all his radiant plans were possible.

When he left the steamer's deck in New York he felt vitality in the new land. Men worked with speed and bustle and direction. The Old World of his youth and young manhood knew nothing like it. As soon as he could write his name in English, he became John A. Sutter. He wanted to be one of the busy throng—an American. It seemed the thing to do.

The map of the United States in 1834 is an amazing document today. Wisconsin was still free territory under the Ordinance of 1787. The area which was to be Montana, the Dakotas, Nebraska, Wyoming, Kansas, Colorado, and Oklahoma was also free under the Compromise of 1820. The Republic of Texas was shortly to map its borders along the waters of the Sabine, Red, and Arkansas rivers. From the historic parallel of "fifty-four forty" to the 42nd parallel, the Oregon country was jointly and feebly occupied by the United States and Great Britain. California and Nevada were part of the United States of Mexico. The United States of America was not a large country then. But the convincing Swiss adventurer was to aid its leap from sea to sea.

Cities did not hold what John Sutter sought. He wanted the virgin land. The towns and surrounding acres belonged to men who had come before him. He pushed on to the then-existing Indian frontier, Missouri. At St. Louis he heard much of the prosperous Santa Fé trade. The traders themselves were indisputable proof of their own yarns. The sight of Missouri land in winter did not please him and he determined to try the Santa Fé caravans for a time.

Sutter drove his store-on-wheels from Independence, Missouri, with one of the Santa Fé wagon trains in the spring of 1835, following the lure of profit south and westward. For three years, until 1838, he was a successful trader. Twice he sent money, small sums, to his family. With the money went vivid letters of a home that was soon to be for all of them.

In Taos on one such trading journey Sutter heard his first reports of California. The French-Canadian alcalde of the town, Popian, told the yarns. He was salesman enough to sell his story to the young trader who was dreaming of pleasant lands.

In April, 1838, Sutter sold his trading gear and animals and made plans to reach California via Sonora. Sir William Drummond Stewart, a shrewd Scot of his acquaintance, advised him to use the Oregon Trail. Stewart believed it was a much safer route for a small party and Sutter took his advice.

Eight men left St. Louis with him in April. They used horses and pack animals only. For safety they depended on speed—they were too small a command to dare pitched battle in case of an Indian attack. For food they had to rely on what they could find along the trail. Captain Dripp, one of the group, was a partner in the American Fur Company and bound for the Wind River rendezvous of the trappers in the Rockies.

First they traveled over prairie and river. Their luck held through cloudburst, buffalo stampede, and Indian attack. Forty-one days out of Independence they rode into Fort Laramie, fur-trading outpost in the Black Hills. Before them lay ravines and heat and hills and the Great American Desert. An hour later they were in their saddles, going on.

The trail rounded Independence Rock and passed the Devil's Gate, a gap in the granite that swallowed up a river. One noon they reached Captain Dripp's goal in the Wind River Mountains. The rendezvous was a temporary post which existed only a few weeks in the year, where the frontier clans gathered to exchange furs for lead, powder, rifles, and knives. Among the thirty or more trappers about the crude blockhouses, Sutter met Kit Carson with an Indian boy to sell. Sutter bought him for a hundred-dollar beaver order on the Hudson's Bay Company. It was a stiff price, but the boy spoke Spanish and English.

The gathering pounced joyfully on Sutter when they heard he was California-bound. It seemed to them a profitable idea to sack the mission churches and run off herds of horses and cattle from unprotected ranchos. Sutter was hard put to discourage these friendly offers without offending the trappers. "Them there Mex critters can be driv' to Orrygon an' sold," argued one of the bearded circle. Most of the listeners were disgusted by Sutter's lack of initiative. The expedition finally left the rendezvous without unwelcome additions. They still numbered eight; the Indian boy rode in Dripp's stead.

The trail continued through South Pass to find Pacific Springs—across the continental divide. Two springs sparkled there within a stone's toss of each other. The waters of one flowed west to the Pacific; the other flowed east to the streams emptying into the Gulf of Mexico.

Jim Bridger's fort was not yet built and the party did not turn to the left. They rode by the basin of Green River to its source, to Soda Springs, and on to Fort Hall. Francis Ermatinger, the commandant, argued against Sutter's plan to strike south and overland to California.

"So small a party is sure to meet trouble," he

SUTTER'S FORT

warned. "These savages are always hostile, always on the lookout."

"What then shall we do?" asked Sutter.

"Keep on to Fort Vancouver," he counseled. "It's a better plan. Winter isn't far off. Snow and cold are as deadly as Indians in a strange country."

Sutter shrugged, nodded.

The path kept to the south bank of the winding Snake until it crossed the river at the present Glenn's Ferry in Idaho. They reached the Boise and went down it to Fort Boise at its mouth. Payette, the officer in charge, furnished a guide to take them over the Snake and Malheur and up and over the Blue Mountains. From Fort Walla Walla they pressed on to The Dalles and its Methodist mission. Ten days later they reached Fort Vancouver.

Sutter had been six months on the journey. He had hoped to find some outbound Hudson's Bay Company boat that would touch at a California port; either that or try the coastal trail. No vessels, he found, were sailing to his destination in the near future and winter was about to make the overland route impracticable.

However, the Hudson's Bay Company bark *Columbia,* carrying a cargo of lumber and furs, was ready for departure to the Sandwich Islands. Sir James Douglas, in charge at Fort Vancouver, gave Sutter permission to book passage. Many trading ships touched the islands en route to California and the prospect pleased him better than a winter spent at the fort.

But his companions thought it was too roundabout a course for them, decided to wait for spring and good trails. Only one, an expert German cabinetmaker, agreed to the trip. The Indian boy went too; he had no choice in the matter.

The islands were a miracle to John Sutter from the moment the *Columbia* skimmed past Koko Point and into the spacious, shallow bay of Waialae, skirting the coral reef, Diamond Head looming near, on past low-hutted Waikiki, a pilot bringing them safely in to Honolulu—"Quiet Haven." His first concern was always the land and under his eyes were colors and odors and tropical intensities strange to a man who had been born in Kandern, in the grand duchy of Baden. At the dock he met Pelley, head agent of the Hudson's Bay Company in the islands. William French, a prominent merchant, was there also. During the first small talk Pelley mentioned casually that Captain Gorham H. Nye had sailed only six hours earlier in the *Bolivar* for California. To Sutter's excited query about the next sailing the agent was uncertain.

"Three or four months, probably," he guessed. With that Sutter had to be content.

His personable manners soon won him friends. He attended functions and met Governor Kekuanoa and strolled the Nuuanu Valley and looked out over the Pali and speculated ceaselessly on ship arrivals and departures. Time dragged.

Three months went by as he fretted. Then an idea gripped him. Swinging on a hawser in the harbor was the English bark *Clementine*. She was open for charter and no one had made a bid for her. He began to interest French, Greenway, Reynolds, and other island merchants in a trading venture of his devising. He proposed to freight the *Clementine* with produce and articles that could be shipped without spoilage, sail to Sitka, barter with the Russians, and finally sell the remaining cargo at California ports. He offered to advance a share of the outfitting cost, sail with the vessel, and act as supercargo without pay. William French was invited to accompany him and take over the financial management for the interested merchants when he—Sutter— left the bark in California.

The scheme went through. The Russians represented an exceptional market and there seemed little risk in the undertaking. Contracts were drawn, the ship chartered and laded with the necessary supplies.

With the voyage assured, Sutter turned to other matters. Three small brass cannon were purchased out of his lessened Santa Fé profits and stowed away for later use in the wilderness. The German cabinetmaker found an industrious countryman who wished to join them. Then the governor offered to supply ten Kanakas —two with their wives—who were willing to go to California for a three-year period at a salary of ten dollars a month. Sutter guaranteed them a return passage and food, clothing, and shelter during the time they were bound to his service.

In April, 1839, the *Clementine* was ready. Captain John Blinn, her hard-faced Cockney master, declared her seaworthy. The sailing brought a host to the wharf. One man brought along a huge bulldog that had been underfoot around the house and presented it to Sutter a moment before the lines were cast off. United States Consul John C. Jones, Pelley, Stephen Reynolds, Abell, McClure, Cheevers, and an added score of well-wishers were there. Even the smiling Governor Kekuanoa waved a fat arm in aloha. One slim-hipped girl threw a lei about Sutter's neck. More white flowers fell on the deck.

Sutter called farewells until his friends grew smaller and the land grew misty.

Sitka, too, gave cordial greeting. Governor Ivan Koupreanoff, colonel in the Garde Impériale of the Russian Navy, was a cheerful cosmopolitan, fierce-whiskered, soft-voiced. He had use for his visitor's cargo of fruits, sugar, molasses, salt, paint, oil, and other stores. While trading was in progress Sutter and French and Blinn were guests of his Excellency in Baranoff Castle where, it was said, when nights were dark, the wraith of Baroness Mary Wrangell walked, calling on her dead lover, a scarlet mark over her heart where she had stabbed herself. A dinner was given in the visitors' honor and there was dancing in the high-ceilinged ballroom and gaiety and fellowship and wine.

In the few weeks of his stay, Sutter not only made a minute inspection of the great post of the Russian-American Fur Company, but grew to know the official family that ordered its affairs. The acquaintance proved invaluable to him later, when because of it he was able to purchase Fort Ross on credit at a time when Russia's southernmost colony had come upon evil days.

Russian guns boomed a salute as the *Clementine* sailed from Sitka. She was starting on a dreary voyage. Tall seas crashed against the bark. Winds tore at her canvas, snapped cordage, and strained the masts. She beat southward and saw no other sail.

Governor Koupreanoff had traced a copy of Sir Edward Belcher's survey for Sutter, the chart Sir Edward had forgotten to duplicate for Vallejo. Without it there is a question whether Captain Blinn could have found the entrance to the Golden Gate where the tides swirled through the rocky headlands.

Slowly they worked the bark through the channel into the port. They passed a dilapidated, dismantled fort to the right. Beyond the ruin they sighted a square of huts—the Presidio of San Francisco.

Before them lay a huge stretch of untroubled harbor, sheltered from the winds by a rising slope of hills. A littoral of open plain was dotted with a score of dwellings. The *Clementine* dropped her anchor close to where the dozen buildings of Yerba Buena straggled on the shore, the village that was one day to be San Francisco. It was July 1, 1839.

7

John Sutter had come to a pastoral land settled by people adept at lighting firecrackers under each other. Everyone owned and enjoyed a grievance. Native Californians were infuriated by the presence of convicts and cholo soldiers sent from Mexico and by dishonest Mexican officials who came regularly to collect and disburse provincial funds. Veterans in California military service hooted at Mexicans dispatched to the territory with preferred commissions. The landholding Californians detested the interlopers, called them "de la otra banda." The Franciscans, many still loyal to Old Spain, had been systematically ousted from their posts by the organized brigandage of secularization; the new administrators, usually members of prominent californio families, were busy taking the mission holdings for themselves before the gardens, vineyards, and herds became valueless from neglect. Deserters and trappers continued to be problems for mañana officials.

Sutter's ship arrived only a week before Mexican

President Bustamante confirmed the appointment of Mariano Guadalupe Vallejo as comandante militar of California and his nephew, Juan Bautista Alvarado, as governor. Long before the *Clementine's* coming, mutual friends of the two aspiring candidates had been riding horses to death in a hectic compaign of bearing tales. The fact that Vallejo in Sonoma sat glaring at Alvarado in Monterey was an oblique stroke of fortune for Sutter.

The *Clementine's* official welcome at Yerba Buena was not what had been hoped. Nathan Spear, the leading merchant, and John Wilson, a brother-in-law of General Vallejo, made a friendly boat visit, but Juan Prado Mesa, military commandant, demanded that they sail at once to Monterey for a port-of-entry permit. They were forced to leave, although the storm-battered bark was hardly seaworthy.

At Monterey, two days later, Sutter laid his plans before the newly confirmed Governor Alvarado. The one-time choir boy and customs inspector was thirty years old and a trifle smug over his recent advancement. His father had been Sergeant Francisco Alvarado, a patient, unlettered plodder who had demanded that the soldier-schoolmasters teach his son to read and write and cipher. Later, Governor Sola had given the boy a chance to improve his penmanship at a clerk's desk in the gubernatorial office.

Young Juan had two comrades them—José Castro and Vallejo. Recently the trio, aided by other californios and a nondescript party of mountainmen, had driven the Mexican Governor Gutiérrez from his post and taken over the governmental offices. This late news of official appointment from the Mexican government was particularly pleasing to Alvarado: he had expected trouble and the possible arrival of another hated Mexican appointee to take over his duties.

He weighed Sutter's words politely, scanned the sheaf of letters his guest had brought. It was the custom of the time to come laden with such missives and Sutter had an imposing stack of them: Popian, Sir William Drummond Stewart, Sir James Douglas, John C. Jones, Colonel Ivan Koupreanoff, and others attested to the bearer's good character and ability.

The governor was interested. The fellow actually wanted to go inland to colonize a river valley wilderness that promised nothing in Alvarado's eyes. But he might be useful.

"Announce your official intention of becoming a Mexican citizen," said the governor reflectively. "Then go inland. Select any tract that suits your fancy. Return here at the end of a year and I will give you your naturalization papers and land grant at the same time. A little paciencia on your part—and it is done!"

The delighted Sutter hurried back to Yerba Buena. Alvarado, too, was pleased. No one had yet gone inland to make a home much beyond the sound of the surf. The valley was given over to Indians, robber bands, and wild animals. Here was a chance to establish a permanent rancho in the very center of a savage district without personal risk or expenditure. It was a clever move to have an ally in that region, reasoned the governor. Vallejo, the Fox of Sonoma, might be watched— possibly even checked in his autocratic rule over the northern bay area.

But Sutter had plans beyond the governor's fancies, and Alvarado would have been less satisfied with his own adroitness had he even suspected them. The Swiss wanted land distant enough from any Mexican military post to discourage a close inspection or any interference with his undertaking. He was planning a private empire, even if the heart of it was to be a home. He wanted a navigable river and a fertile valley. Rumor told him where he could find both. So he said little and bought supplies and looked over two craft open to charter.

Sutter planned to make two short trips before he went up the river. He wanted to meet Vallejo, at Sonoma, and Rotscheff, Russian governor at Ross. Friendly neighbors are a useful commodity to a stranger with ambitions for a wilderness conquest.

He made his visits. Vallejo was courteous, even helpful. Rotscheff and Sutter liked each other on sight. But Vallejo's smiles meant nothing and it was Rotscheff who proved his goodwill in later days.

The trading firm of Nathan Spear and William Sturgis Hinckley was appointed as Yerba Buena agent of the colony-to-be. From them Sutter chartered two small schooners, the *Isabel* and the *Nicolas*. The agents also agreed to supply him with all the agricultural implements, tools, provisions, and needful gear. In addition, a small four-oared pinnace was purchased outright to give the wilderness site an active carrier between bay and valley.

The three small brass cannon that Sutter had brought from Honolulu were stowed carefully aboard the little fleet by the Kanakas. A few deserters about Yerba Buena talked themselves aboard ship under the doubtful eye of its owner. In the dawn of August 9, 1839, the start was made. Nearly every Yerba Buena resident was on hand. Most of the well-wishers had been attending a going-away party given in Sutter's honor on the *Monsoon,* then in port, and they staggered on deck to wave leavetakings as the colonizers stumbled into their river craft.

Sutter stood in the bow of the pinnace. At his feet squatted the bulldog given him in Honolulu and the Indian boy from the Wind River rendezvous was beside the dog. The Kanakas bent their brown backs and the oars flashed. The dawn wind began to whip the *Isabel* and *Nicolas* on their way.

That night the party landed near Rancho Pinole and Sutter arranged with Don Ignacio Martínez to furnish him with horses and sheep and cattle as soon as a messenger brought word that a permanent site had been selected. Payment was promised in beaverskins or produce in a year's time. Sutter's funds were gone. His share of the *Clementine's* profits had not been available in cash. As was the California custom, he had been promised hides and tallow the following season. Already he was indebted to his Yerba Buena agents for half his present equipment. But he had a supreme faith that the wilderness would pay well for its conquest, and soon.

For eight days the fleet made its tortuous way, exploring the banks, making side journeys in strange delta waterways, fighting mosquitoes, seeking signs of good land beyond the tree-bordered Sacramento. A few miles below the present site of California's capital city they met their first challenge from the valley Indians. A hundred painted savages shot arrows from the shore until Sutter, talking to them with a runaway mission neophyte as interpreter, promised them gifts at his next landing.

Shortly the three vessels came to the spot where the American River joins the Sacramento. They veered

right at Sutter's command. A few miles farther on, the
country enchanted him. A lush valley bordered the
stream, level and pleasing, stretching on to distant
ranges. The river itself was broad and navigable. Herds
of deer and elk grazed on thick grasses and high trees
grew in the green expanse.

It filled John Sutter's land-hungry eyes. "Here!
Here is a likely spot!" he cried. "Pull in! Pull in!"

They landed, tied up the boats, and pitched their
tents. Supplies and freight were shifted ashore. The
three cannon were mounted and put in order—nothing
was certain or secure in this new place.

The savages came for their gifts. Trinkets were
passed into their brown hands. The sun sank beyond the
red mountains in the west, leaving Sutter to sleepless
campfire visions. His feverish mind saw orchards and
yellow grain in the sun and a tiled home sitting on the
valley sward. Anna's voice in the home; young voices
in the orchard. . . .

In the morning the deserters who had joined him
lost their zest for wilderness life. The savages looked
too many and the wilderness too vast. With no ceremony they rushed aboard the *Isabel* and *Nicolas* before
the two ships began their return voyage to the bay.
Sutter fired his cannon as a salute to the departing ships
and turned to the work at hand.

He found a knoll not far from the riverbank that
caught his fancy and moved his camp there the second
morning. Shelter was needed and he set mission-trained
Indians to making adobes, dancing and yammering on
the mud and straw. The Kanakas scurried about and
raised three grass huts. More Indians were set to work
hacking a way through the chaparral to the embarca-

dero. Back went the pinnace and crew to Rancho Pinole for the promised cattle, with instructions to drive the herds overland. They rowed their way into Vallejo's displeasure and were delayed by official orders, much to Sutter's chagrin and rage. It marked the first breach between the two. Sutter's cattle, decimated by ill-luck, did not cross the Sacramento until late October. The small force left at the camp was nearly wiped out by a night attack, Sutter escaping only because the faithful bulldog sank his jaws into an Indian's throat. These were days of peril, though only an indication of the hazards to come.

Adobe making was slow. The forty-foot square structure that Sutter designed, with its blacksmith shop, kitchen with fireplace, and personal living room, rose slowly. It was barely thatched with tules before that first rainy season came, a torrent that sent the river over its low banks, made the valley first a quagmire and then a lake dotted with islands. The islands sheltered shivering herds of elk and deer and wild horses, huddled there to keep from being carried away in the surge of waters. Sutter's herds stood belly-deep in water in their improvised corrals and only the insignificant hill offered any refuge from the seething expanse.

But work went on. Trees were cut and dragged to the blacksmith shop. Furniture was sawed and put together. Iron plows were fashioned to take the place of the crude California variety—only branches of trees with fire-hardened points had been used before John Sutter's coming. Other tools were sharpened or welded in entirety. During the downpour the pinnace did not attempt the voyage to Yerba Buena for three weeks. But Sutter did not complain. "A great country for

moisture," he remarked laconically to the German cabinetmaker who had joined forces with him. That uncomfortable artisan had another and more profane
description for it.

But it ended. With spring the waters fell back
below the riverbanks and sank into the rich earth. An
emerald glow appeared where the liquid expanse had
been. Ground grew firm under the feet and seed was
sowed. More white men began to trickle out to the
colony in 1840 and Sutter's Oregon Trail comrades
sought him out after an overland journey from Fort
Vancouver.

At nights now, by candlelight, John Sutter sat
before his table, a sheet of paper under his fingers.
Carefully he traced a rectangle and set down dimensions
in precise script. It was the plan for Sutter's Fort, the
first stronghold in the interior of California, capital of
the Great Valley's second empire, and a refuge for
Americans for the next decade. His pen sketched slowly.
The fort was to be 500 feet long and 150 feet wide;
the walls were to be 18 feet high and 3 feet thick.
Bastions would overhang the walls at the southeast and
southwest corners, commanding the gateways in the
center of each side except the western. Loopholes would
pierce the walls at intervals and there would be an inner
wall with the intermediate space roofed over and par-
titioned for shops and manufactories. Other detached
buildings were sketched inside the enclosure: living
rooms, granaries, and workrooms. While the camp slept,
John Sutter drew his careful lines.

In April the citadel was begun. Letters to Anna
and the children took on more buoyancy. He made
horseback trips about the vicinity, spying out the land.

He met Don Antonio Suñol and John Marsh and got cattle from each on credit. Beaver trapping was begun. Plans were made to turn wild grapes into brandy. The Indians proved troublesome once more and were taught another bloody lesson. Gradually those who lived on the neighboring rancherias discovered that the new Lord of the Valley would protect them against attackers from near or far. Mission-bred outcast or gentile, they came to depend on Sutter as a benevolent, impartial force, to be feared only if he was treated as an enemy.

Indians who worked for him were generously paid. A tin currency was set up in the land which Sutter called New Helvetia, for his fatherland. Coins were stamped out by a blacksmith and a star cut into each. A disk with one star meant one day's work, and so on. These were distributed to the Indians who had no present needs. Later, if they wanted shirts or tools or food, the coin's equivalent in goods was passed out to them.

As months sped by, Sutter won himself Mexican citizenship and a captain's commission in the Mexican Army; became, by Alvarado's appointment, the official magistrate of his inland empire. A grant of eleven leagues, seventy square miles, was given him. Trappers and homeseekers from America began to come to his fortress as a haven. His power grew with each day. He purchased Fort Ross and Bodega from the departing Russians on his promise to pay $30,000 in installments of produce and cash and brought all the furnishings from his two purchases overland or by the river to add to New Helvetia's glory. With the sale he acquired a "copper-bottomed, copper-fastened" schooner which he renamed the *Sacramento*. All the Russian coastal lands were added to his empire. Hock Farm, his great Feather

River cattle rancho, was laid out and then improved. Phelps and Ringgold and Emmons and de Mofras and other travelers were to speak of his goodwill. His hospitality was a wilderness legend and no man paid for it.

8

Although American trappers had been pushing restlessly up and down the river valley since Jedediah Smith's coming, the first official visit was made by an "Around the World United States Scientific Expedition" which actually did sail around the world regardless of precedent. For four years—from 1838 to 1842—Lieutenant Commander Charles Wilkes led the first party of this kind ever to sail under the Stars and Stripes. And this expedition was the first to map and explore the Sacramento River, by land and water, from its source to the Pacific.

Wilkes's six warships were stowed to the hatches with scientific gear and specialists to use it. The young republic wanted all the information it could get about the rich, unexplored lands of the earth. It was hoped that the expedition would come back with valuable data. Wilkes piloted his ships into many places where he wasn't much wanted, but his scientists made charts and took notes anyway. The tender *Flying Fish,* her bottom rotted by pounding seas, was sold in Singapore. The sloop-of-war *Peacock* was wrecked in the Columbia River in July of 1841. But the *Vincennes, Porpoise, Relief,* and *Sea Gull* carried enough stout Yankee luck in their timbers to circle the globe safely. The expedition even bought a ship in Vancouver, renamed her the *Oregon,* manned her with the stranded crew of the *Peacock,* and joined her to the fleet.

The *Vincennes* dropped anchor in the bay off Yerba Buena in 1841. A month earlier, a ship's cutter under Captain W. D. Phelps had sailed up the Sacramento beyond New Helvetia, the first craft to carry the American flag on the river. Lieutenant Commander Cadwalader Ringgold of Wilkes's expedition went upstream in August with a half dozen ship's boats. He and his party stopped long enough to be John Sutter's guests on an elk hunt before rowing on as far as they could take the boats. Then they made their return on a placid, sun-dappled stream early in September and carried their reports to the rolling copy desks aboard the *Vincennes.*

Meantime another party from Wilkes's command, officers and scientists and seamen, had begun to explore the river from the north through the Willamette Valley. Young Lieutenant Robert Emmons, who liked a good joke with his meals and was impatient with all guides, was in command. James Dwight Dana was the geologist, A. T. Agate the artist, and Surgeon Whittle the wit of the party. Baptiste Guardipii was the current guide whom Emmons suspected darkly of imbecility. Added to the group, for their safety, were a number of families bound for Sutter's Fort, among them Joel P. Walker, his wife, and children. Mary Young Walker was carrying in her arms her seven-month-old daughter, Louisa, the first white child born in Oregon of American parents. And Mary Young Walker, when she arrived at her destination, found herself the first American woman to reach Sutter's Fort.

Emmons began his journey in early September and it took him a dangerous month to pass through the country of "Bad Indians" before he finally made camp under Mt. Shasta. Immediately a friendly band of Indians visited the camp anxious to trade their bows and arrows for trinkets. Their yew bows of feathered, close-grained wood and reed arrows with obsidian heads were marvels of good workmanship. The quivers of deer, raccoon or wildcat skins also brought a fair price in American knickknacks. Joel Walker put up a button as a target and one Shastan hit it three times at twenty paces. The grand prize for the competition was a piece of tobacco.

Emmons wrote that these Indians "were a fine-looking race, much better proportioned than those to the northward, with their features more regular and expressive. One bare-legged boy was extremely good-looking. He had a bright, black eye, a pleasing face, and he was clad in dressed deerskins that fell gracefully over body and shoulders."

For five days the party followed the course of the Upper Sacramento, amazed at the number and swiftness of the creeks that joined the river, and fascinated by the thick forests, the great, ragged crags of Castle Rocks, by the "chalybeate spring" in the green valley beside the stream, and by the animal and bird life to be seen everywhere. The horses grew sleek and fat and the tension known in the perilous Oregon Indian territory vanished. Walker recalls that Dana told him: "This is truly a golden stream!" Naturally Walker recalled it years later. I doubt if the geologist had any proof that the river was a "golden stream" except for the few nugget specimens he found along the way, even though his reports to the government were highly prophetic of the days to come.

On the fifth day of pleasant river travel they found the tumbling Pit adding its volume to the Sacramento, not knowing that a few miles to the east the McCloud had entered the Pit. They passed from the hills into the Upper Valley and here Guardipii justified Emmons's faith in him by losing the way. This delighted the lieutenant, who was further amused when Warfield's Indian wife pointed out the right trail without hesitation.

From the highlands of fir and pine they had come to where sycamores and oaks and cottonwoods shaded the water. Genial and docile Indians visited the camp in the evenings, laughing and curious. Sometimes their dark hair was drawn back behind and held in a knot by a deer sinew. Beads dangled from their pierced ears. Some had painted blue-black triangles on their cheeks as an added decoration. Emmons noticed them eating fish and pine seeds and grapes and venison and wildfowl of all kinds. He saw them pound acorns into pulp and then flavor the mixture with arbutus berries and a little water to make it palatable. Only the men came to the camp, so Emmons made it a habit to visit the rancherias, where the women did all the work and the men danced or gambled.

Emmons took his party from the Wintun rancherias down the western bank of the Sacramento, finally fording it at a spot they named Bear Camp, where Inass, one of their Indian hunters, killed a grizzly for meat. When they saw Prairie Buttes—Sutter Buttes today—rising sharply out of the plain they camped near a creek called by trappers Little Fork of the Buttes. Here, only a year earlier, Michel La Framboise and his men had taken a hundred beaver in a day. Close about the volcanic buttes they found the ground covered with the bones of wild animals that had been too late in seeking safety in the highlands when the river was in flood.

Soon they reached the Feather at its junction with the Sacramento and camped in an oak grove. The Feather was so high and swift that it was two days before they could cross safely. Near the ford they saw an Indian burial ground, marked by a towering mound of skulls and bones, "said to be all that remains of a great tribe, done to death by an obscure disease."

Next day they came to John Sutter's fort and rested. Emmons, Dana, Agate, and Surgeon Whittle, with their jumbled notes and sketches, went back to Yerba Buena on the *Vincennes'* launch. The others went by land, Emmons assuring them with a raised eyebrow that no doubt Guardipii would be able to lead them the rest of the way without faltering.

Emmons charted the Upper Sacramento as Destruction River, perhaps because he confused it with the McCloud, from which Alexander Roderick McLeod had carried a story of hard luck back to Vancouver. The Sacramento has been a highway of many names. Padre Narciso Durán supposedly gave it the name it bears today. Moraga called it the Jesus Maria. The trappers named it the Spanish River. Some called it the Bonaventura and some just the River of the North.

9

In April, 1840, nearly every American in California was thrown into prison. Within three weeks seventy of them were on board ship, heavily ironed, on their way to San Blas. By the end of May they lay in

Tepic Prison, half-starved, dirty, and covered with vermin.

The seizure was as startling as it was unexpected. No foreigner suspected such a move; that is, no foreigner who was not later accused of having had a hand in the plan. The captures were made so quickly that no news traveled to the sections ahead of the arresting squads.

Reasons for the tempest were trivial. Alvarado and Vallejo were always worried about turbulent aliens. Isaac Graham, a cantankerous Tennessee mountaineer who had aided Alvarado and Vallejo in the 1836 revolt, was given to tall yarns and threats when under the influence of his own Natividad distillery product. It was rumored that he had made some significant statement to the effect that he had placed the governor and the general where they were; and that he could just as easily unseat "them thar garlic-hounds."

This rumor was enough. Secret preparations were carried out. Imprisonment and banishment was the result for Graham and many others. Naturally there were exceptions. A few Englishmen and Americans who had become Mexican citizens were unmolested, notably the popular, respected merchants.

Only one spot was not touched. There was no interference with Sutter's citadel and its isolated position was not the chief cause for this immunity. There were guns and ammunition in the Sacramento Valley. Captain Sutter was an imperious man and quite likely to protect his stronghold. It was suspected that he could control the Indian tribes and might even be able to use them in case of invasion. Diplomatic necessity forced Vallejo to forget that the inland empire builder existed.

The plight of the Tepic prisoners prompted angry exchanges between official Mexico and the United States. In less than six months they were released with apologies, given passports, and presented with small sums to ease their feelings. Many of the exiles returned and most of them nursed a grievance against the men who had banished them. Some of them found an outlet for that grievance six years later when they faced Vallejo at Sonoma and gave him a taste of prison life.

Open enmity had existed between Vallejo and Sutter ever since the general had delayed the herds bound for New Helvetia late in 1839. The latter sent a blunt note to Sonoma at the time accusing Vallejo of a deliberate intention to starve out the new colony. No written answer reached the fort from Sonoma but Vallejo wrote his brother, comandante at San José, angrily calling attention to the fact that "we must not lose sight of a settlement of foreigners in the direction of the Sacramento, said to have been made with the permission of the departmental government, yet contrary to the law and the latest orders from Mexico. The establishment is very suspicious."

Shortly after the roundup of foreigners in 1840, Sir James Douglas, once host to Sutter at Fort Vancouver, sailed into San Francisco harbor bent on two errands. In addition to Hudson's Bay business he wanted to investigate the possibilities of Britain's acquiring control of the Sacramento region. Both his party and Sir George Simpson's later expedition were intended to create pro-British sentiment in the province. Both were aided by James Alexander Forbes, the British consul, and Michel La Framboise, leader of the Hudson's Bay trappers in the region.

Douglas was irritated now at Sutter's position. The Swiss held the key to California: from his valley and with his help the thrusts of American conquest might strike. Sutter was in conflict with English ambitions for both commercial dominance and territorial expansion. He had even ordered La Framboise and his crew to stop trapping in the valley. Douglas called it insolence; went so far as to question Sutter's authority in the disputed area. Sutter ignored him.

Douglas then tried to enlist Vallejo's support. The general pointed out that Sutter was within his supposed rights and inquired, equably enough, just why Douglas expected the right to trap the section anyway? The Englishman knew a stone wall when he saw one. But before he sailed back to Fort Vancouver he bought a building and installed a company agent in Yerba Buena. It was a headquarters for whatever action England might take in California, commercial or colonial.

Sutter's first season, with its downpour, should have meant a bumper crop. But he had few plows and a limited supply of seed. So the yield was small. The second season of 1840-1841 was one of drought, as was the third season of 1841-1842. Only enough seed was threshed that third year to replenish the seed that had been sown. Less patient men would have given up.

But there were some compensations. Trapping in 1842 was much more successful than in the first years. More traps were either purchased or made by Sutter's blacksmiths, more hunters were employed, a greater variety of goods was kept on hand to bring the free trappers to the fort for trade, and Michel La Framboise and his roving band were so harassed by Sutter's threats and commands that they made little inroad on the valley supply of pelts. In increasing numbers beaver and land-otter skins were piled in fort storehouses.

Don Antonio Suñol supplied the colony with distillery equipment. Wild grape brandy of good quality added itself to the list of exports. Deer fat and hides and tallow were sent by boat to the bay region. Sutter began to pay off Don Antonio and his Yerba Buena creditors with pelts.

In 1841 emigrants were cutting ruts in the parched plains and snapping axles in the mountain passes on the way west. A few went to Oregon, but most of them came to Sutter's Fort. Many stayed there for a time. Some were later important in California's story: John Bidwell, Charles Flugge, Bartleson, Chiles, Thomes, and lesser names. Talbot H. Green was to find success and, years later, be discovered as a man of mystery wanted in the East—not Talbot H. Green at all. Most prominent was to be Bidwell, the young New York schoolteacher who became Sutter's right-hand adviser. Few emigrants came in 1842. But it was only a pause.

Sutter was fast expanding the occupation of his huge Mexican grant beyond Hock Farm and the fort. He had installed Nicolaus Altgeier at a site on the north side of the Feather River. Between the Feather and Yuba rivers he had leased an area to Theodore Cordua, a corpulent, whist-playing crony. John Sinclair was in charge of Eliab Grimes's rancho on the American River. William Gordon, "Uncle Billy," was settled on Cache Creek.

Others who served him faithfully were given outright gifts of land. They were buffers against intervention, Mexican or Indian, and they dovetailed admirably into Sutter's schemes. Sutter saw to it that their sense of security and property ownership was identified in their minds with the stability of New Helvetia.

"I am no stronger than the men who surround me," he confided to the astute Flugge one night, before blazing logs in his quarters at the fort. "By Jupiter, if we give a man land he's a homeowner, not a trapper! He'll fight for his home. That means he'll fight for New Helvetia. This is a common venture, Herr Flugge."

Sutter's unexpected purchase of Fort Ross in 1841 was a triumphant coup. Both Vallejo and Sir James Douglas had bid for the Russian holdings. But Rotscheff's friendship and Colonel Ivan Koupreanoff's memory of his visit to Sitka gave Sutter possession of the Ross colony and all its equipment. The contract was approved by the Russians without even a down payment.

The Russian-American Fur Company for some time had planned the virtual abandonment of the post. Furs were growing scarce along the ocean and in the Farallones region. The venture had never shown a profit, even in its first years when the Aleuts were most successful as hunters.

Sutter wasted no time after Russian sails sank beyond the horizon. Everything within the walls of Ross was rushed aboard the *Sacramento* as fast as it could be stowed away. Indian vaqueros rode overland with the Russian cattle to be added to New Helvetia's herds. Even the fort walls were pulled down and taken inland. The work of removal went on through 1842. Out of the ruin of Russian hopes Sutter was determined to raise an impregnable stronghold in the valley.

In the midst of this task news came that the Honolulu firm of French and Greenway had failed and that

Sutter's entire profit and investment in the *Clementine's* voyage, overdue, would never be paid. Sutter took time out to swear and then went back to work.

Commodore Thomas Ap Catesby Jones actually conquered California for the United States in 1842. In September, Jones happened to be in Callao with three ships. Out of the harbor before his watchful eyes sailed an English fleet, under sealed orders. Almost within the hour Jones came upon an item in a New Orleans newspaper asserting that Mexico had ceded California to Great Britain for $7,000,000.

It looked as if the British fleet was up to mischief. Jones dragged up his anchors from the harbor bottom and put to sea in thirty minutes.

After a hurried conference with his officers, the commodore sent the *Dale* to Panama with a report for Washington because he was sure that Mexico and the United States were at war. Crowding full canvas on his two ships, the *Cyane* and the *United States*, he laid his course for the California coast.

For months the British and American fleets had played a game of watchful waiting up and down the Pacific sea line, each anticipating orders to take possession of California. Jones had no intention of allowing Admiral Thomas to raise the Union Jack over the disputed soil. He hoped, grimly, that he wasn't too late.

The *Cyane* and the *United States* captured Monterey on October 20th without burning an ounce of powder. Terms of occupation were arranged in friendly fashion and the Stars and Stripes fluttered proudly over the castillo at eleven o'clock on a clear, hot morning. Juan Bautista Alvarado was still in charge of the departmental government but he had cautiously removed himself to his Alisol rancho when he saw the first sails rising from the sea.

The commodore landed in person next day and rummaged through port archives. With some amazement he came upon late dispatches of a very disturbing nature. In the comisario's office he found a document dated August 4th that explicitly declared no state of war existed or was imminent.

With growing anxiety Jones sat in his captured town and pondered. The situation was puzzling enough and most embarrassing. Here he was with a captured capital and no reason for taking it. Regretfully he made a decision. No war, no capture.

Combining due ceremony and hasty apologies he delivered the town back to the Mexican officials, who were even more puzzled than he. Jones had been master of Monterey for exactly thirty-six hours. Down came the American colors and the Mexican flag waved again over the castillo and its rusty cannon.

Sutter shrugged when he heard the latest news. "American occupation will come anyway," he said. "I hope it will be soon." And word of his chagrin was not long in reaching Sonoma.

10

Political popguns exploded in the valley once more in 1842. Mexico was determined to raid the California fruit basket again. As customary, a Mexican had been appointed for the task. Vallejo and Alvarado, who had handled all the departmental worries since their successful revolt, had also handled the revenues. This had gone on long enough.

Colonel Manuel Micheltorena was the new official designated as governor, comandante militar, and inspector of California. He was scheduled to remove the two native Californians from the seats of power. Naturally they determined to prevent it.

In August, on his cross-country inspection tour to Monterey, Micheltorena arrived in San Diego with three hundred soldiers. After being feted by the San Diegans, he moved on to Los Angeles a month later. Just before his arrival there, General Vallejo had an idea in Sonoma. Posthaste he sent a messenger with a letter to greet the newcomer. The governor was advised to march at once against Sutter's Fort with all his command. Sutter, reported Vallejo, was harboring a vicious alien element. If California was to be long held, he and his colony must be driven out and his citadel laid waste.

Sutter knew what was in Vallejo's message before Micheltorena received it. He was intimate with certain "foreign gentlemen" who knew Vallejo's plans. Vallejo's sisters had made it a habit to marry American merchants and this did not help the general keep his schemes secret. Sutter, too, wrote a letter to the approaching dignitary and sent it by the resourceful Charles Flugge. In it he pledged his personal co-operation as "comandante militar de las fronteras del Norte y encargado de la justicia," congratulated the colonel on his appointment, and declared, briefly, that any previous dispatches received by his Excellency were without foundation. In closing, he offered to appear immediately before the governor upon his arrival at Monterey, delicately hinting that news of some importance was being reserved for his private ear at an appropriate time.

Flugge brought back to the anxious Sutter a

friendly answer which carried an invitation to call at Monterey at his own convenience.

The governor was angered, however, when he learned of Commodore Jones's capture of Monterey, and its return to Mexico. He wrote Jones about a final indemnity. He would accept fifteen hundred complete military uniforms, the number which he insisted had been ruined by his forces on the march to Monterey— his three hundred men having presumably worn out five uniforms each. In addition he demanded $15,000 to reimburse the Mexican treasury for expenses incurred in meeting the "invasion"; and finally "a complete set of musical instruments to replace those ruined on this occasion." Politely puzzled inquiries about the last demand revealed that patriotic Mexicans, as they thundered upon lost Monterey, blew so hard that they burst their horns.

Sutter described the mounting unrest to a group of his cronies as "a very hot stew." And he was right. The uncertainty of tomorrow made every valley dweller suspicious of his neighbor and gave credence to rumors never fathered by fact.

In the new year, 1843, Michel La Framboise and his men did not return to the valley. Sutter was delighted and put forty of his own trappers in the field. Deer suet, brandy, salmon, sturgeon, beaverskins, landotter pelts, and rifles purchased from incoming emigrants were sent to the colony's creditors. Three hundred cattle were sent under Robert Livermore's supervision to Don Antonio Suñol as an advance on the amount due him. The Russians kept patiently sending their vessels to collect the annual installments due on the Fort Ross purchase, even bringing iron, agricultural implements, and other supplies to New Helvetia. Their boats went back without the wheat Sutter had promised: three arid years in a row left him no choice in the matter.

Yet much as Sutter sent to the majority of his creditors, everyone was not satisfied. Threats were made and tart words were spoken—at a distance. Sutter kept his placid courtesy; at least in ink. He assured the interested parties that the next year would see all deficiencies wiped away in entirety. Actually, he saw the future bright. His faith in the new land never wavered.

At one time or another in 1843 nearly every settler in the valley came hurrying to the shelter of Sutter's Fort. There were stories hinting at a repetition of the 1840 arrests and imprisonments. The scares were groundless. No force in the province could have dared such wholesale seizures. But the uncertainty made the valley people restless and started agitation for a new government that could assure order.

Sutter made his first visit to Micheltorena after one of these rumors had disrupted fort routine for two weeks. He found the governor cordial and co-operative, quite willing to make land grants to various deserving settlers, ready to guarantee their lives and property rights under the Mexican law. Sutter came back from his trip with a new ally and news that foreigners were not being expelled. His assurances calmed the valley and made friends for the governor which he soon needed badly.

Though 1843 was the third arid year for New Helvetia, 1844 promised much. Rainfall was normal. Sutter made plans to seed an immense acreage, using hundreds of fanegas of wheat—each fanega weighing 133 pounds.

Half a thousand Indians labored in the fields and more, under Sutter's direct eye, worked on the fort walls. The order was that they must be finished by autumn.

The annual matanza—slaughter—was held at Hock Farm in July. With the grass green, feed was plentiful; cattle were fat and heavy. The novillas—steers—averaged two hundred pounds of meat to each animal; this was dried and the rest left to the buzzards and wild beasts. When very fat the steers produced one hundred pounds—four arrobas—of tallow to an animal as well as two arrobas of manteca, the delicate home-cooking fat much prized by californios, which lies between hide and ribs.

John Bidwell was in charge of Hock Farm that year. Under his direction there was less lost motion than in the usual native matanza. Hour after hour the try-pots bubbled with the melted sebo and manteca. The sweating vaqueros worked with the hides, preparing them for market. Most of the tallow went to South America to make candles and soap. "Boston ships" would transport the hides back to the East from San Diego, carrying from thirty to forty-five thousand skins packed tightly in each hold.

Events in the colony moved smoothly and profitably. More good traps were hammered out by Sutter's blacksmith and more furs were caught in season.

Peter Lassen, whose name adorns a high peak today, was busy under Sutter's patronage in manufacturing some home furniture that had been ordered by Don Antonio Suñol. The seventeen-ton *Sacramento* was wrecked on a salvage trip to Fort Ross and took fifteen days to repair. From his hattery, Sutter exchanged hats for soap with Don Antonio; also bridles, made in the leather shops. From the tannery, built on the riverbank near the spot where Sutter first landed, came an increasing amount of good leather. His Indians were turning out blankets and shirts from the blanket factory. Military drill was mandatory for natives near the fort or in the fort employ. Brandy grew better and more plentiful. Whist games continued, if Sutter was at home. In April, Thomas Oliver Larkin, United States consul at Monterey, wrote and asked for all data on incoming emigrants for the year. Sutter had a good report to make.

Two parties arrived, one of thirty-six people, the other of a hundred and fifty. Granville P. Swift, William Bennett, and the Kelsey family came in the first company. Patriarchal Elisha Stevens led the other, which included Dr. John Townsend, Allen Montgomery, and the Murphys—fifteen of them.

In 1844 John Charles Frémont fought his way down through Sierra snows to the fort, leading a United States Topographical Expedition on his first journey to California. Frémont, then a young second lieutenant of engineers, wanted to be the first man to make an accurate mapping survey of the Far West. But, during the midwinter, Sierra drifts had almost spelled disaster. Dog meat and mule meat was the only food the men had in the last few days before reaching the valley. Only John Sutter's speedy aid and his willingness to re-equip Frémont's entire party of thirty-nine saved the expedition from destitution and probably Mexican imprisonment. Food, clothing and animals were cheerfully given to Frémont. His reactions were not notably friendly. Petulant about details, he was demanding and arrogant in his dealings with Sutter, and later, with Mexican officials

and rancheros. After resting at the fort awhile, Frémont pushed on, returning to St. Louis the same year.
But he came to California again in 1845.

In October of 1844 dissatisfaction among the californios had increased because of Micheltorena's policies.
Alvarado, Castro, and their friends did most of the
grumbling. Once more the word went from rancho to
rancho that "the despicable tyrant thus throttling all
California liberty and honor must be driven out!" That
the governor was not entirely responsible meant little.
The revolt was the thing.

Sutter rode overland to Monterey the same month
and secured further proofs that all land titles would be
guaranteed in the Sacramento Valley. To preserve New
Helvetia he was quite willing to uphold the accredited
government against californio insurrectionists. In return for a promise of military aid which he made
Micheltorena, he was given what was termed a general
land title. With this in his possession he was empowered
to issue his own grants to those settlers who applied to
him for land and who had previously conformed to the
necessary Mexican regulations. That power made Sutter
feel considerably more secure, not only for his own
huge holdings, but in accepting the land claims of others
under Mexican law.

The revolting forces made the first move on November 15, 1844. A party of fifty Californians under
Pico, Castro, Chávez, and Rico drove off the government horses from Monterey to the Salinas Valley. They
seized arms and ammunition cached at San Juan
Bautista and set about rallying the people to their cause.
Alvarado immediately joined the insurgents.   José

Castro was appointed commander in chief, a decidedly doubtful honor at the moment.

Vallejo was cautious. To be on the winning side in every argument requires an artistry not always fully appreciated by one's contemporaries. He hedged a bit; it was better not to join the revolt openly until events had shaped themselves to his liking. Micheltorena, as his superior officer, had already ordered him to send reinforcements to aid the government. To avoid this, he disbanded his military forces on the plea that he could no longer carry such a financial burden at his own expense. His soldiers at once joined the rebels, as he knew they would.

The governor marched from Monterey against Castro and called for Sutter's help. On New Year's Day, 1845, Sutter came to his help with two hundred and twenty men, a command gathered from the valley settlers and trappers. The rebels retreated south with the combined government troops in pursuit. On the way, Micheltorena legalized Sutter's second grant, the Sobrante, adding twenty-two leagues to his empire.

In the San Fernando Valley, their ranks trebly strengthened by Los Angeles rancheros, the insurrectos defeated Micheltorena and Sutter at the comic opera battle of Cahuenga. Both men were captured and the governor forced to abdicate.

For a day Sutter expected to face a firing squad at any moment. Tempers were short among the victors. One expedient presented itself to him. As a captain in the Mexican Army he had been ordered by his superior officer, Micheltorena, to join him in the field with military aid. He had done so. He produced the written order from his saddlebags. Now, since a new governor, Pio Pico, already elected by the insurgents, was in command, he was perfectly willing to transfer his allegiance to the new official government.

Pico, Castro, and the others pondered his defense and finally released him. They swore him to uphold the new regime and confirmed him in his old rank. But he was still five hundred miles from the Sacramento with nearly two hundred men unmounted and practically weaponless and foodless, dependent on his leadership. The Mexicans had firmly refused to return any equipment taken from the prisoners. Sutter was without money and he could get no credit.

He struggled back as best he could, through Tejon Pass to the Tulare Valley and on, avoiding hostile Indians, swimming rivers, living on the wilderness. It was two weeks before he rode through the gateway of his citadel. An hour later he remembered the date. "A proper Fool's Day," he muttered. It was April 1, 1845.

I I

Two hundred and fifty more Americans who wanted rich lands to settle came overland to California in 1845. James Wilson Marshall arrived with the McMahon-Clyman party in July. No doubt Lloyds of London would have wagered odds of a million to one that Marshall would never show the world where to find more than a billion gold dollars. And Lloyds would have lost.

Among the year's emigrants were others important to California's future, from gangling Robert Semple, who was to help start California's first newspaper, to

William B. Ide, who rode under the Bear Flag. Most of them found work in the shops at the fort.

Valley crops were magnificent that year. Sutter's Indians began to reap the high, plump-headed wheat. Some used scythes, some butcher knives, others the sharp edges of split willows. After the grain was cut it was carried from the fields by groaning two-wheeled carts, carretas, to the eras. These were Russian-made threshing floors of redwood planks, brought overland from Fort Ross, and the only ones in the province. All the Mexicans threshed their crops on hard-packed clay ground.

The eras were bulwarked by an eight-foot fence of redwood planks. A gate opened inward upon the wooden floor. From the carts the grain was thrown to a two-foot depth on the smooth-planked surface. Brood mares were turned in on the wheat and Indian vaqueros drove the animals in a circle. The plunging mares circled the platform, dizzy and snorting, stamping the wheat underfoot while the cloud of straw dust shimmered like a golden mist in the sun.

At intervals the vaqueros rode in front of the mares and stopped them short so the wheat was turned bottom-side up under their sliding hoofs. Again and again this performance was repeated. Each time the mares were stopped they were started again in the opposite direction. After an hour the grain was threshed, the straw shredded into chaff. Shovelfuls of the flattened mixture were thrown as high as brown arms could toss them into the breeze. The chaff blew away but the kernels fell vertically downward, to be gathered later. The grain was stored in granaries near the mule-driven flour mill. Out of the crude mill came a well-ground flour, ready for fort ovens.

Enough grain was left over to send a sizable cargo back on the Russian brig *Baikal* in October as a payment on Fort Ross. It was the first shipment of any magnitude that Sutter had been able to send.

The fort gardens were filled with berries and swift-growing vegetables. Indian squaws labored each day, tending the long rows and loamy beds. Continually, they irrigated with water carried from the near-by pond at the rear of the fort. Long lines of natives carrying water could be seen, hour after hour in the summer months, going from the pond to the vegetable rows. Lettuce, carrots, turnips, potatoes, peas, cabbage, parsnips, beans, and melons came in season from the valley beds.

This year so propitious to John Sutter's fortunes brought no tranquillity to California. Well-paid and dignified positions were not numerous enough to suit the insurgent leaders. Pio Pico as chief executive and José Castro as comandante militar had sidetracked Alvarado into the post of administrator of customs at Monterey. This was a bitter pill for the ex-governor. Another innovation incensed the northern Californians: the capital was moved to Los Angeles.

In November, Captain Andres Castillero, a Mexican commissioner, arrived at Sutter's Fort accompanied by José Castro. They offered Sutter a hundred thousand dollars or the mission lands of San José in their entirety in exchange for his Mexican grant and "improvements." This was Mexico's move to win Sutter's Fort without force of arms and stamp out the active threat of American invasion which it represented.

Sutter refused, politely. His choice was America and he believed it would take California. He didn't think Mexico had a hundred thousand dollars in cash anyway. Money was still scarce and his pockets were empty. Creditors were demanding. It was twelve years now since he had left his family. Mails were slow and uncertain. But he felt he would soon be able to have Anna and the children with him. He reflected that they were hardly children any longer. The years had run fast.

In December, 1845, Frémont again reached Sutter's Fort. It is improbable that on this expedition he carried actual instructions from Washington to effect the military occupation of California. But officials doubtless hoped he would be in a strategic position, if trouble came, to turn his party of sixty men into an invading force.

Once more Frémont was hospitably received and equipped at the fort. After a few days he rode on to join the portion of his party under Edward Kern which had entered the valley through Walker's Pass. With his entire command he proceeded through the Santa Clara Valley without official permission.

The passage of this armed group of aliens over Mexican territory started trouble. General José Castro inquired pointedly of United States Consul Larkin in Monterey just what this mysterious expedition meant. Then three of Frémont's men battered their way into Don Angel Castro's home during his absence, made improper remarks to his flashing-eyed daughter, Mercedes, and tore the bodice of her dress in a scuffle. On the very heels of this incident Frémont sent an insulting note to Castro in regard to a horse-stealing charge made against his men. Castro tartly ordered Frémont to leave the country. Frémont refused and then climbed up the side of Gavilan Peak. There he raised the Stars and Stripes over his camp, and awaited Castro's next move.

The general promptly marched against the peak with two hundred men. On the night of March 9th Frémont fled in the darkness. He raced back to Sutter's Fort and started on to Oregon. But he was overtaken by Lieutenant Gillespie, bearing dispatches from Washington. Evidently Frémont's previous instructions to "act at your own discretion" were amplified. He hurried back to the Sacramento and camped near Sutter Buttes.

Near these hills the Bear Flag Republic came into existence on Frémont's advice. About him had flocked what John Bidwell terms "the floating population around Sutter's Fort." These men were ripe for mischief that promised profit and diversion. A few still remembered Tepic Prison. There was a scattering of reputable frontiersmen among them, but in the main this drift of men about Frémont was unstable and unscrupulous.

A party of thirty-three men, nominally commanded by Ezekiel Merritt, advanced from the buttes on Vallejo at Sonoma. The force arrived at dawn, June 14, 1846. The general was aroused to find his home surrounded by a band of leather-shirted trappers, raucous in the sunrise. Vallejo, his brother Salvador, Victor Prudon, and Jacob Primer Leese were made prisoners and carried inland to the rectangular fortress where John Sutter had already hoisted the American flag. At Sonoma the crude Bear Flag flapped in the wind, banner of one of the briefest republics in human record.

Frémont rode with ninety men into the still astounded hamlet and its garrison of trappers on June 26th. A few days later three Californians were shot down at his order because he "wanted no prisoners." They were the de Haro twins, Ramon and Francisco, and the older José de los Berreyessa, owner of the Santa Clara rancho. All were unarmed and, having landed from a small boat, were approaching Mission San Rafael. News of these deaths ran from rancho to rancho like a great wind. Could any peaceful californio expect more consideration than those who died at San Rafael?

This Bear Flag incident was not significant, but it achieved a great deal of ill-will. Without the seizure of Sonoma, it is reasonable to think that annexation of California would have come without bloodshed. The majority of natives, fed up with continued disputes, would have welcomed United States rule to guarantee personal safety and property rights. If Sonoma had not been captured, the province might have been won as peacefully as Monterey was taken by Jones four years earlier.

Commodore Sloat captured Monterey on July 7th. Lieutenant Missroom of the United States Navy lowered the Bear Flag at Sonoma on July 9th and ran up the American colors in its stead. Three days later Funtelroy and a squad of United States dragoons hoisted the same flag in San Juan. Thus, in less than a week, every town in northern California came under American domination. It seemed, for a time, that the San Rafael deaths and the swift military occupation would stir no determined opposition.

Frémont moved on to Monterey. The energetic Commodore Stockton arrived on July 15th to supersede Sloat. Yet the American position was not secure. The conquest was not yet completed. Even with the aid of every American settler and trapper, men were few. United States warships were undermanned because a large proportion of officers and crews had gone on shore to fight. A clash with Great Britain over the Oregon country was a possibility. American ships with skeleton crews could never have withstood a swift English attack. Stockton demanded speed to prevent any prolonged resistance by retreating californios.

But Castro and Pico were finding the going a bit rough. With mutual accord they took flight from Los Angeles on August 10th and went by separate routes to Sonora. Stockton and Frémont, joining forces, marched unhindered into the town. Not a shot was fired. The two leaders congratulated themselves that the conquest was complete. Stockton remembered that six American presidents had been interested in acquiring California. John Quincy Adams first gave it his attention. Now James Polk had lived to see the old dream a reality.

Immediately a semimilitary government was set up. Frémont was named military commandant of California. Monterey was again chosen as the capital. Gillespie was stationed in Los Angeles with fifty men. Stockton sailed back to Monterey, sure that a civil government could be set up at once.

In the north, too, a new government took over. Washington Bartlett was appointed alcalde at Yerba Buena. An election was held there that brought out an unbelievable voting strength of ninety-nine people.

Meantime Frémont was returning overland to Sutter's Fort. En route he stationed Lieutenant Talbot and nine men as a temporary squad to hold Santa Barbara. Only a show of force was necessary. All resistance was over.

Then out of certainty leaped disaster. A group of hotheads among the southern Californians began the Second Revolt and drove out Gillespie. He had been trying to enforce a nine-o'clock "curfew law" on californios who were not conditioned to stomach such trivia. Forced to evacuate Los Angeles, Gillespie embarked with all his men on the merchant ship *Vandalia* on October 4th. Nearly every male Californian in the south joined the new revolt. The wildfire movement took on purpose, something new in californio wars.

Frémont and Stockton hurried back to the lost area. Fifty rebel horsemen under Flores raised a dust screen by pulling bushes over the dry ground and held Stockton in check "before superior forces" for a week. Colonel Philip Stephen Kearny, rushing to the conquest, galloped into the transparent ambush at San Pascual and the deadliest encounter of the campaign. John Bidwell, chased out of San Diego with his garrison, lived on the ocean for some weeks, cruising up and down the coast, keeping out of harm's way and hoping for the best. Mervine's sortie against men born to the saddle had its climax in the American graves he dug on Dead Man's Island.

It was all a good show, with a trace of comic opera even in its harsher moments. Flores, chief leader of the southern revolt, was sometimes not more than half a stride ahead of his pursuers. And Doña Flores draped a golden shawl over her husband as he crouched on the floor and sat over him while she invited Frémont's raiding party to search the house and talked French fashions with the officers. For four months the southern Californians held Kearny, Stockton, and Frémont at bay before they surrendered. It was not until the first month of 1847 that the Second Revolt ended and Gillespie once more doggedly raised Old Glory over Los Angeles.

The restive Vallejo had spent long weeks in duress at Sutter's Fort before his release. At twenty-eight he had been comandante general of California, a ruthless politician ably insulated against friendship and generosity. He never forgave Sutter his courtesy nor Frémont his harshness during those days of imprisonment. He was not yet the amiable person of his later years, nor the self-educated, book-loving Spanish-Californian he subsequently became.

The American flag flew in California and a new order was shaping. Talk of statehood was heard from the Sacramento's banks to San Francisco Bay and military regulations were posted from bulletin boards and tree stumps. Yerba Buena became San Francisco, but the most drastic change was to take place in the foothills. To John Sutter it was to matter more than to all the others.

PART THREE

Gold

I

FOR ten years after it was discovered gold dominated the history of California. Then, in Civil War days, when the harvests taken from gravel and quartz began to lessen, the fertile land showed itself to be California's future. During the forty years that led into the new century the once free grass of the cattle ranges was fenced; the great herds disappeared and the grainfields came; new settlers arrived by the hundred thousand whom gold had not called; markets and railroads prospered; and the grainfields changed into vineyards and orchards which heralded the intensive farming of today. But, in the decade when gold was king, a story runs fiercely—gold and the machine against the land. . . .

2

Young Jerry King stood on the rolling deck of the *Sabine* as her anchor dropped down into San Francisco Bay and thought of a girl walking demurely down the green lanes of Boston in the spring. The girl had copper hair and a tilted nose and lips that were always crinkling with laughter and eyes that were as blue as a smiling sea. He wondered what she was doing now and how she looked and if her eyes were starry with remembrance of him. Jerry King hardly saw San Francisco as he waited for the ship's boat to lower away. His goal lay beyond this village, out there over the bay horizon in America's newest valley lands where a man could build with the strength of his two hands something that was real and secure against the years, something a man's sons could make a little better and hold in trust for their sons. It was worth fighting for, thought Jerry King. And he set it all down that night in a red-lined book that would have been a ledger if it had stayed in Boston.

As the ship's boat beached and the baggage-laden passengers scrambled ashore, it pleased young Jerry King to forget the last hundred and sixty-eight fretful, bedbug-bitten days aboard the *Sabine,* now bobbing behind him on the tide. They had left Boston on the last day of September, 1847. Now it was midafternoon of March 16, 1848.

A club-footed runner for the Colonnade House wheeled most of the *Sabine's* passengers and their luggage to Kearny Street, a few doors from Portsmouth Square, Jerry among them. Dust rose in clouds from the rutted streets. Jerry saw merchants in frock coats, Guayaquil hats, and velveteen breeches, Indian women in gay prints and moccasins, sailors with tattooed arms, and Mexicans and californios, all sartorially aglitter. Creaking oxcarts drew supplies to the various stores. Dogs and mules blocked every corner. There were United States soldiers in the throng, emigrants from overland, and even a few trappers, overawed by the large town of eight hundred people, wandering watchfully here and there.

After leaving his few belongings in the cubicle Messrs. Conway and Westcott called a "room of the first class," Jerry went out into the town again to buy supplies. He went alone. None of his fellow passengers was going inland yet. But Jerry was in a great hurry. He wanted to start for Sutter's Fort the next day. Conway of the Colonnade House had spoken about the fertile acres of that rich region.

Jerry had a short list of things he wanted. In Robert Parker's Adobe Store he found a hatchet and boots. At the Bee Hive he bought two pounds of "Fine Hyson Tea" and five pounds of flour. At Mellus and Howard's he picked up a side of bacon, a saucepan, and a bucket. At Davis's he bought a frying pan. He made this suffice for his outfit because goods were expensive.

A gangling trapper in fur hat and leather jacket and breeches was leaning against the side of Davis's store as Jerry came out. He had a knife and a pistol in his belt and his right arm was draped about a long rifle. His moccasined feet resembled large hams covered for transportation and his leather-brown face had a grin on it.

"Gittin' prettied fer the trail, hey, stranger?" said he. "Well, ye'll have good weather fer it. Rains mostly over and not enough wind tuh blow the tar outen a sailor's britches."

Jerry said he was going into the valley.

"Leavin' tomorry meself—kinda crowded around these parts." He shook his furry top piece. "Sure ain't what she used tuh be."

"Where are you bound?"

"Up Cap Sutter's an' Orrygon way."

"How'd you like a partner as far as the fort?" asked young Jerry suddenly.

The leather-faced man squinted good-humoredly. "Glad tuh have ye, young feller. Cap Sutter's launch is leavin' afore sunup—do ye know her?"

MINING OPERATIONS AT
MURDERERS' BAR

"No. But I'll find her."

"Good." The trapper grinned and moved away.

Jerry called after him. "Hey—my name's Jerry King!"

The trapper waved. "I'm Jim Kinnard—Big Foot Jim they calls me." He kept on traveling. "See ye afore sunup, young feller."

Jerry went back to the Colonnade House, his supper, his tallow candle, and the red-lined ledger.

3

The dawn wind had not yet sprung up and the stars were still bright when the *Amelia* began her journey for the Sacramento. Jerry King sat aft on blankets and duffel. Big Foot Jim was beside him. There were a half dozen other passengers, indistinct and mostly silent as the crew of four worked with the sail, the oars, and the tiller. The tide bounced the twenty-ton *Amelia* occasionally as if she were a rubber ball and Jerry braced himself against the roll, peering out to where the shadowy forms of Yerba Buena, Angel and Alcatraz islands stood closer than the Contra Costa shore.

It was an hour before the breeze began to slap the canvas in quick gusts. The sun rode up out of the east into a clear sky and drew the morning chill from the air. Manaiki, the Kanaka cook, passed steaming hot coffee around and talk quickened. An eager-eyed man, with a blanket still draped over his shoulders, was reading the March 15th issue of the *Californian*.

"Did you see about the gold discovery up at Cap Sutter's sawmill?" he asked inclusively.

Most of the passengers shook their heads. "Up Coloma way," he added. "Says it was found in considerable quantities." He squinted back at the paper.

Another man lowered his coffee mug long enough to shake his beard. "Prob'ly not much to it. Takes a powerful lot o' gold to beat good wages."

A general assent was murmured. The subject was shelved for the more interesting one of land and what a man could do with it.

"It sure beats all," affirmed a one-eyed man with a shawl around his thin neck and a tattered frock coat belted about his middle, "how things do grow big here. I seen a squash that weighed tarnation nigh eighty pounds last year—old Yount grew 'er. Ain't nothin' but what grows three-four times as big as anythin' back in the States."

Some of his lately arrived companions were incredulous. Another added a little more weight to a cabbage he had seen. The discussion grew louder and not overly polite.

Jerry and Big Foot Jim did not share in the arguments but drifted into talk of their own. Jim had been with Bill Williams and Joe Walker and Steve Cooper when they had helped survey the road from Independence to Santa Fé with the Sibley Expedition in 1825. "Not that we done the surveyin' fer 'em," he grinned. And he had trail yarns and tales of Taos orgies that fascinated young Jerry King. "Best o' the hull passel, he is," said Big Foot Jim reminiscently of Bill Williams. "Old Señor Sly-Paws hisself when it comes to readin' sign an' he kin grain a skin quicker'n another man kin light a fire." He chuckled at an old memory. "Joe Walker an' Bill Williams an' me an' some other lads come through here in 'thirty-three an' picked up about six hundred horses. They was just jumpin' around without nobody near 'em"—Big Foot Jim's right eye dropped cautiously and then raised itself—"an' we run 'em out through Walker's Pass clean through the Sierry. Got some nice trade outen 'em too." Jim sighed for the good old days when California horses were fair game for honest trappers. Then he resolutely grunted, closed his eyes, and set himself to slumber on his mound. . . .

It was noon of the third day before the *Amelia* nosed her way in to Sutter's Embarcadero. There had been a silver veil of rain that morning but the sun shone for a full hour before the landing.

Jerry and Big Foot Jim made their way toward the fort along the Indian-cut trail, passing sheep and cattle attended by Indian vaqueros. Walking briskly among the shade trees that grew beside the path, they passed through the unguarded fort gate in a cloud of dust set up by an oxcart and found the inner rectangle alive with voices and bustle, the clang of the smithy and the rasp of the carpenter's saw. Two or three Indian horsemen dashed out of the gates on some errand, their horses' hoofbeats almost lost in the din. Mechanics and laborers and traders moved here and there intent on their tasks, hardly bothering to give a glance to the newcomers. A few idle Indians lounged about. The oxcart creaked over to C. C. Smith's store quarters and two Indians began to unload it under the strident direction of a bald-headed, red-bearded white man who appeared to have an excellent command of Indian dialect.

The two walked across to the central building and found a clerk in charge. Captain Sutter had ridden up to Sutterville, his new real estate venture on the near riverbank, and Dr. Bates came into the office as the visitors

were arranging with the clerk for food and lodging.
Bates took them in tow and they went over to his
rooms for a noon meal. The doctor had just heard
some bad news about which he was a little reticent. Tom
Shadden had ridden in with tidings that the outlaw
bands of the San Francisco region were planning to raid

the valley for cattle. Bates felt there was no reason to
doubt Shadden's word. He shook his head occasionally
as they ate. "Have you heard of the gold discovery?" he
asked finally, with an assumption of carelessness.

"It was in the paper," said Jerry.

"There may be something to it," said Bates guard-
edly. "Captain Sutter hopes that it won't hold up work
on the sawmill."

"You mean there's really gold—very much of it?"

"Lots of it," said the doctor, dropping his voice. "If I was a young man I'd go up to Coloma and get my share of it."

"Coloma?"

"Yes. That's the place where Sutter is building his sawmill. The tailrace is full of gold flakes. Everybody here thinks there must be plenty more in the stream beds thereabouts. It should be worth a try."

Jerry shook his head. "I came for land," he said, smiling.

"Plenty of that too." Bates shrugged. "Ask Captain Sutter when he gets back. He needs young men who think like you."

Big Foot Jim joined in the conversation with thick but hearty comment. "No gold 'r land fer mine," he said. "I'll stack what a string o' skins'll fetch agin sweatin' over a shovel 'r lookin' fer somethin' in a mill-race without hair on it." He sighed contentedly and patted his stomach. "Not fer me, pardner. I'm leavin' fer Orrygon by sunup."

4

The days began to move faster for Jerry King. Sutter was eager to give him land on credit if he would promise to work his holdings. But John Sutter no longer had absolute authority in the valley. In late January grumpy Jim Marshall had stooped to finger the first flakes of gold in Sutter's millrace at Coloma. And now California heard nothing but stories of gold, stories that spread a fever over the earth. California life had been based on the three institutions that had made possible the expansion of the Spanish Empire in North America; the military establishment of the presidio, the colonist's settlement of pueblo, and the mission. California was now entering an era in which new institutions supplanted the old.

But it took time. Jerry King was persuaded to be John Sutter's man for a few weeks before he made up his mind about the location of the land he wanted. He saw the gold fever grow daily in the citadel. It increased slowly yet very surely. Under Jerry's alert gaze wagonloads of provisions went to the millrace and, returning, brought a generous sample of Coloma's newly sawed planks. Firewood came in and Indians were plowing cornfields in the early springtime. Visitors came and went with a new purpose: Major Lansfield Hastings from the new town of Montezuma; John Bidwell from a gold hunt; Marshall and Peter Wimmer from Coloma. Launches came and went from Hock Farm and the sheep were sheared. Sutter was worried and went on trips to both Natoma and Coloma millsites. He doubled the workers' wages, spoke of nothing but finishing the mills. The horse mill at the fort broke down and was repaired during one of his absences. Dr. Bates and John Sinclair rode to Coloma "for a look at the gold mines." Jerry watched them depart with a feeling of curiosity growing under his mop of curly brown hair. Sam Brannan and Hawk, the express carrier, sailed in on the *Dice mi Nana* (*Says My Mamma*) on April 6th. Back went Brannan four days later to San Francisco on the same launch, his shrewd brain a heated popcorn hopper ready to explode ideas over the San Francisco streets. A hundred of John Sutter's hides were shipped on the same boat. But Sam Brannan was not thinking of hides in such paltry numbers. He owned a store at Sutter's

Fort and if a "gold rush" could be engineered he was ready to supply ten thousand men with what they needed, at a profit.

Jesse Martin and Sidney Willis came from Coloma with $500 worth of gold to trade at Brannan's store on April 14th. That same evening Dr. Bates and John Sinclair returned with heavy bags of flakes. "We picked it up in ten hours," Bates told Jerry, with a weary gesture. Bates was old and tired and the trip had been a hard one.

That night Jerry sat down and wrote a letter to Elspeth Deyne in Boston. It spoke of a home in the valley, but mostly of gold. "Perhaps I can come for you sooner than I thought, my dearest dear," he wrote. "They have found gold—*actually* found it—near here. With any luck I'll be home very soon with enough of it to keep you in silk dresses for always—even if you insist on weeding our flower garden-to-be out here every day! . . . You will love this new country and we'll make it what we want it to be."

It was a hasty letter, written because "Mr. Gray of Virginia" had stopped that evening at the fort "on his way to carry the express overland to the United States." It was a stroke of great good luck to catch the messenger to the East. Soon Elspeth Deyne would be reading his momentous letter and filling her mind with the glorious, unbelievable news it held. Miracles *did* happen. He could almost see the blue eyes sparkling above the tilted nose and her fresh, young lips crinkling into laughter. It was good to be alive and in love. And young Jerry King set it down unashamedly in the red-lined book that had begun a life of adventure, quite aloof from its figure-filled fellows in Boston counting rooms.

From then on it was easier to read the fever signs. Major Pierson B. Reading and Edward Kemble, editor of the *California Star*, arrived on the launch *Rainbow* on their way to the Coloma country. Hardy and Dickey and Bidwell and Coates followed them. Knight and Nash and Gendron and Sicard quit their land and their duties at the fort and turned their faces to the hills. The country was changing. Digging for treasure does not make for placid shoveling or home building or lawmaking or crop growing. Jerry grew increasingly restless. On May 4th he joined Dr. Bates. The land could wait.

Now, for the first time, "holes" began to appear in Jerry King's ledger entries. Working all day and then sleeping, dog-tired, in blankets under the clouds or stars, left little time to write down daily items. Jerry had left a frantic Sutter watching his workbenches and stores and fields deserted for the hazardous road to swift fortune. By mid-June San Francisco, too, was a lifeless place, with three citizens in four ranging the foothills, coming by river and trail with a mounting and consuming certainty. The gold area began to expand impossibly. Men thought they saw gold in all the streams and began to scatter like hunting dogs confused by ten thousand scents.

Jerry had some luck in the Coloma region. But he did not stay long. He tried Mormon Island and his pack load grew heavier with treasure. Later, at Bidwell's Bar, a tattered fragment of the *California Star* came into his hands, passed on by a newcomer from the bay. Editor Kemble was in dark mood over the condition of California. "The whole country from San Francisco to Los Angeles and from the seashore to the base of the

Sierra Nevada resounds to the sordid cry of Gold! GOLD! G O L D !" he wrote. "The fields are left half-planted, the houses half-built. Everything is neglected but the manufacture of shovels and pickaxes and the means of transportation to Captain Sutter's Valley." What Jerry didn't know was that as soon as the worthy editor wrote and published that statement he shut up shop, paid a high price for a shovel, and started for the same place.

Navigation companies began an exploitation without an equal since. Steamship lines were formed for both the Cape Horn and Panama routes to San Francisco. Every ancient hulk available was jerked into dry dock, calked, daubed, painted, and renamed to become a stanch new steamer. Newspapers were hired by boat owners to print lies about the gold yield. Huge pieces of iron were gilded and displayed in windows and showcases in nearly every city and village in Europe and America. These exhibits bore the artfully brief title: "From California." Crowds jostled to see the fabulous finds. No man could pass by without knowing discontent and determination at the same time.

Speed was the idea. Get there before the other fellow. Heaps of baggage labeled or tagged "Sutter's Fort, California" choked the ports of the world. It was suddenly the most famous spot on the habitable globe.

In the East men gathered and made plans to organize caravans of covered wagons for the overland trip. A rash of popular "stock companies" appeared all over the world. These stock companies were financed at so much per share by the members: officers were elected, passage supplied, rules enforced, trading supplies carried, and agreement reached on how to distribute the wealth communally acquired. Even stay-at-homes could buy a share interest and await the return of more adventurous neighbors weighted down with treasure to be divided.

Sometimes these companies took their names from the cities or towns of their origin. The Golden Hive Mining Company of Bordeaux was a French venture. From Boston the *S. L. Crowell* carried the twenty-one members of the Holyoke and Northampton Mining and Trading Company. The Hope Mining Company, twenty-two strong, sailed from Nantucket on the *Fanny*. The Rough and Ready Overland Mining Company left New York on the steamship *Greyhound*, fifty aboard. With the same number, the Massasoit Mining and Trading Company of Lowell, Massachusetts, sailed from Boston in the schooner *Harriet Neal*, but between Chagres and Panama these gold hunters put up a shack and sold hot doughnuts to passers-by. After all, ships for California were scarce on the Pacific side and hundreds of clamoring men were ahead of them. Why not make a penny while waiting for passage?

When the snows fell in the Sierra and the rain soaked the valley, Jerry King came back to Sutter's Fort. He had $4,000 worth of gold in three pokes and he knew that when the snows and rains were gone again he would find more. He worked for the plagued Sutter, who was finding it easier to get mechanics and helpers while the mountains and streams were impassable and the "diggings" incalculably cold and dreary and death-breeding. Cholera was skulking about too. Many miners were hurrying back to San Francisco, a city no longer deserted but growing lustily with each hour, looking for comfort and pleasure.

Jerry sent his gold off to Elspeth Deyne with long notes about clothes and furniture. It cost him an outrageous price to send it but it spoke of riches in the land and he wanted her to see that all the shining tales were true.

The fort was busier than ever during that waiting-time. Miners and traders and drovers and Indians came and departed ceaselessly. Every storehouse was jammed to the ceiling with merchandise and all the shops were rented or given over to fort business. Sutter's personal quarters were crowded each day with visitors who wanted something and he found it difficult to say no. And Jerry himself was counting the days until the spring rains would end.

Jerry left the fort again in late February of the new year—1849. The tide of forty-niners from the East and foreign ports was beating in to add a violent temper to the hunt. The early comers had known each other before the fevertimes, had lived by a rough code of justice and square dealing. Now criminals rode into the country, vandals eager for gold no matter how it was acquired.

Jerry found a "pocket" on Burley Creek in April. In four days he took out $18,000 in dust and nuggets. At dawn of the fifth day he was riding his horse toward Sutter's Fort, saddlebags half as heavy as himself. He had made up his mind. He was going back to Elspeth Deyne. And then they were coming, as fast as they could, back to California and a new home. He could see himself, staggering under his heavy find, and Elspeth's astonished loveliness as she opened the big white door!

He rode with a fine, careless air that morning.

It would be easy to work the land with the help of the gold in the heavy bags. He was doubtless singing as he rode. He wrote once that he continually sang the songs he and Elspeth had sung together back in Boston. If ever a man had reason to sing on a sun-bright morning, Jerry King did.

A gun snarled in a thicket and young Jerry King never knew when a leaden pellet blasted the life out of his brown eyes. He fell with his face in the rich dust and he lay as if he slept, with his brown hair all tumbled and his young eyes wide on a distant scene. . . .

It was so John Coberly, of Oldtown, Maine, found him. John Coberly was new to the gold fields. Most men would have passed the dead man by. Time was precious. Better to sink a shovel in golden gravel than dig a grave. But John Coberly set himself to digging beside the trail.

A little red-lined ledger had been tossed beside Jerry King by someone looking for other things. Coberly picked it up and thumbed it over. Then he put it in his pack. It had a name and address on the flyleaf and Coberly promised himself gravely that he would return it to Jerry's people. There was a small tin case lying beside it, a daguerreotype likeness. The picture was so misty that John Coberly could feel none of the beauty of Elspeth Deyne. Yet its fading lines had always been clear to Jerry King.

Then John Coberly filled in the shallow grave and placed stones over it to keep wild animals away. On a piece of tin taken from his pack he punched holes with an awl until one could decipher the name: Gerald King. He nailed the metal square to a log and set it over the mound of rocks. Adding the daguerreotype to the red-lined ledger in his pack, he went his way.

5

In 1848 with a hundred Indians and Kanakas to do the work, Sutter had hunted gold along the South Fork of the American River and later at Sutter's Creek. John Sinclair had used Indians for the same task on the North Fork. So had Charles Weber, founder of Tule-burg that became Stockton. Major Pierson B. Reading commanded scores of Indians on the streams at the northern end of the valley and across the summit of the Coast Range. But with the coming of the hordes in '49 Indian labor was declared taboo. Every newcomer felt entitled to the gold he could gather with his own hands; he had no intention of allowing anyone else to use a hundred hands to enrich one man. It was the American individualist speaking. Even communally organized "stock companies" disbanded within a few weeks of reaching the gold fields, each member streak-ing for pay dirt "on his own." A stock company dedi-cated to sharing the gold found by its members usually "lasted as long as a tallow cat in Hades," to quote one miner who had come by sea and isthmus with such a party.

Trying to find the right answer for each problem as it came, John Sutter set himself to cope with this tide. But the storm was brewing for Sutter. Miners were moving up to Mormon Island, Kelsey's Diggings, Yankee Jim's, Rich Dry Diggings destined to become Auburn, Weber Creek, Hangtown, Murphy's, Angel's Camp, Jamestown, Wood's Creek, and all the others.

The City by the Gate came first, if you were headed for the Sacramento and the valley foothills. San Francisco was a tented camp as strangely luminous after dark as a dream city. In daylight life was a harsh scramble among merchants, gamblers, and criminals trying to annex the miners' gold before it could be shipped eastward. Prices were pushed high and then higher. Sometimes gold was worth only $14 an ounce at the "diggin's," but $16 an ounce in San Francisco. That lured the miner in, but once in city streets the average man didn't keep his "strike" long. Gamblers paid as high as $10,000 per month for floor space and made reasonable rents impossible. Sometimes $5,000 was wagered on the turn of a card, with a record as high as $20,000. As soon as ships arrived, every man on board started for the mines. Sometimes cargoes lay in the vessels to rot. A forest of masts began to spread over the bay area as hundreds of craft lay crewless, creaking on rusty anchor chains. Rats half as large as terrier dogs infested the town, ate as much flour and bacon as the citizens, fought in the streets, and made forays from ship to ship in the bay by swimming. Wharfs were pushed out over bay mud as enterprising owners competed for business. Crude hotels charged what they could get for accommodations. Eggs were $3 each. The price of a meal was proportionately fantastic. Mountains of goods and perishable supplies lay about in unguarded heaps, lacking storage room. Much of this material was unusable because eastern merchants often sent shiploads of silks, huge plate-glass mirrors, satins, elaborate furniture, and what not to a California direly in need of shovels, picks, trail clothing, boots, and food. Tons of wire sieves, rolls of sheet lead, barrels of spoiled

Peruvian beef, and other unwanted impedimenta were used to pave muddy streets in the rainy season and give a firm footing to men and dray horses usually hip-deep in ooze. There was great fluctuation in all prices from day to day. Plank toll roads began to stretch to outlying tents and shanties over the sandy hills, so that goods could be transported in any weather. Humorists had signs stationed at intervals along these wooden thoroughfares: "Swim Here Without Charge"; "No Bottom at Twenty-Five"; "Dray and Driver Lost Here"; "Through Passage to China"; "Good Fishing for Mudhens Below."

The American military governors of California, Philip Stephen Kearny, Richard B. Mason, and Bennet Riley, did their best for the territory over a period of three years of constant flux. The men of '49 brought murder and robbery after the comparatively orderly existence of '48. Plagued by deserting soldiers and sailors, carried along by swift events, these military governors could do little to curb the raw strength of the current.

With the need for mining supplies and transportation to the diggings, towns rose up along the Sacramento and its tributaries. They came into existence if a determined individual sitting in a single tent on a bedroll, a crisscrossed paper in his hands, could persuade the prospective buyer of "city lots" to believe that marts of trade would soon surround the real estate dealer's "central edifice." New York-of-the-Pacific was largely a paper city on Suisun Bay, frowning at Robert Semple's Benicia on the opposite shore. Up the river, Onisbo fronted the mouth of Steamboat Slough. Webster luxuriated on the eastern bank of the Sacramento, with Sutterville standing some miles above, John Sutter's bid to recoup the lessening importance of the fort as a place of outfitting and departure to the mines. Washington was built on the western bank, opposite Sutter's Embarcadero. Lieutenant Cadwalader Ringgold of the Wilkes Expedition had returned to found Boston on the northern bank of the American Fork, a venture swallowed up by Sacramento City today. Up the main Sacramento, Colusa, Butte City, Placer City, Monroeville, Tehama, Laodecia, and Red Bluff burst into miraculous, if shadowy existence.

The Yuba, Feather, and American rivers and their creeks had their share of "cities." Beyond Ringgold's Boston on the American came a second Washington City, Springfield, Vernon, and Vermont. On the Feather, Nicolaus Altgeier had founded Nicolaus. Between Nicolaus and the Yuba, just below the mouth of Bear River, lay Oro. Plumas City sat at the mouth of Reed Creek; El Dorado City lay opposite Hock Farm; Eliza blossomed a few miles north. Nye's Ranch became Marysville, two miles above Eliza, with Linda a mile farther on. Yuba City was only a mile from Marysville up the Feather. Above Linda, on the same stream, lay Columbia, Oakland, Featherton, and Veazie City. Bidwell's Bar stood where the Feather tumbled out of the mountains. Near by, Oroville, Lynchburg, Oregon City, and Hamilton were "rival cities." Survivors of these "towns on paper" are few today. Most of the names exist now only in histories. But they represent the go-getting, speculative spirit of the time.

John Sutter Jr. staged a dramatic entrance at Sutter's Fort in late 1848 and began to help his father. He alone had come. In April of the next year, with funds at last at his disposal, Sutter sent one of his employees, Heinrich Lienhard, to Switzerland to bring Anna and the rest to California. But they did not reach Hock Farm until 1851.

John Sutter's great hope was statehood for California. He felt that the law would guarantee his land and his future against the gold hunters and squatters. Thousands, like him, lifted their voices to demand an end to uncertainty, but not with the same idea in mind. Some of them were sure the law would not give one man all the land John Sutter claimed.

With the summer of 1849 the men who had returned to work in Sutter's shops during the winter months began an exodus. In April only two remained, a blacksmith and a wagonmaker. Then they, too, walked away to the diggings.

Leather lay rotting in the tannery vats. Anvils gave out no clang. Saws stood with dulled teeth and hammers lay unused on benches. No wanderers reported for even a few hours' work.

It was confusing to John Sutter, even though he had a son by his side to help bear the burdens now. The Indians still worked in the fields and tended the herds, but their numbers had dwindled. The looms still ran, but Sutter was not sure how long they would continue to run.

His flour mill was quiet and no threshing was done. Whenever his boats went freighted to San Francisco they came back loaded with eager hordes. A little while before this almost everyone had trusted his neighbor. Now, overnight, no one's property seemed safe.

If a miner needed a horse, he took the first one he saw; more often than not it was one of Sutter's. If a passer-by needed a bullock for food, he butchered a bullock; quite often it was Sutter's bullock. His sheep met the same fate as the horses and cattle. Supplies began to disappear from the fort: nothing movable or usable was safe. Men went to sleep and woke to find that some nocturnal wayfarer had walked off with something he needed or liked.

But there were compensations. Sutter was receiving large rentals for his fort rooms and storehouses. The stores were doing a rushing business in food, clothing, and mining supplies. But all these commodities were brought in by boat, now. Sutter's shops and fields and mechanics did not produce them.

He reasoned that men must eat, wear clothing, own shovels and rockers and pickaxes. He opened stores at Coloma and Sutterville. Because he needed help, he chose partners who seemed to him trustworthy. Some of the newly arrived drift were smooth-spoken gentry. They insinuated themselves into Sutter's confidence and became his aides.

Wagonloads of provisions went almost daily from the fort to Sutter's posts. During his absence these posts were supervised by his new employees. The foodstuffs and supplies were bought by Sutter at stiff prices from other fort merchants.

Every agent stole from Sutter. His gold flowed out for the wagonloads of goods and failed to flow back from their sale. All the rents from the fort—$3,000 monthly—were invariably overdrawn in advance.

Destitute gold seekers sought him out and asked him to enter into mining contracts with them on shares. He listened and furnished all of them with food and tools. His "partners" profited, win or lose. A gold strike always meant that Sutter's associate vanished in the direction of San Francisco's gaming tables. If they made no strike, they returned for more supplies. John Sutter was simply not emotionally equipped to refuse aid to anyone.

Each trip the *Sacramento* and the *Amelia* made up and down the river realized an immense profit for the owner, regardless of nonpaying passengers on the return. Ferryboat service across the stream was another source of income. Out of the sale of Sutterville and Sacramento City lots Sutter was able to make the final payment on the Fort Ross purchase in early 1849. Claims submitted by the Hudson's Bay Company, Don Antonio Suñol, Martínez, and others were paid without demur. Everything that resembled a debt was wiped away.

By midsummer Sutter moved from his headquarters to Hock Farm on the Feather River. He leased his fort rooms at $200 a month. It was retreat but not defeat. His stock was far safer than at the fort. Everything was transferred: provisions, farming implements, goods for the Indians, animals, and furniture. He even built a new home on the Feather rancho to be ready for Anna and the others when they came.

Sutter wanted more law than that which governed the mining camps of every inaccessible ravine and valley foothill stream. But this first semblance of law in the gold country is a tribute to the common sense of the majority of Americans who took their chances there with picks and muck and rockers and gravel and cholera and quartz rock and shovels. With murder and robbery common, the miners rebelled against the outlaw elements and the parasites. They gathered in a forum, made their own regulations in each camp, elected their alcaldes and sheriffs, and regulated behavior, size of mining claims, penalties, and kindred problems with dispatch and fairness. So excellent a code did these early miners draw up that it exists as the mining law of the land today. But these rules for conduct in the mining areas did not solve John Sutter's dilemma. Each day he spoke more eagerly of the time when California would become a state.

6

The Congress of the United States was finding California a difficult problem. Was it to be a slave state or free? The country hesitated even then on the verge of civil conflict. Opponents of slavery battled fiercely for a measure to declare that all new territory annexed must be free. Slavery groups fought just as fiercely for the exclusion of such a law. There could be no compromise on the flaming issue. The intense struggle on the other side of the continent ended in bitter deadlock and for long months kept California from being accepted as a state.

This critical phase of national dissension stirred resentment in the waiting province. More than a hundred thousand people had come to California within a year of the gold discovery. The Spanish-Mexican pastoral scene was gone forever. Men of goodwill were desperately anxious for order, the assurance of land titles and safe conduct for their persons. These would come, they thought, when California became a member of the Union. They began to demand statehood.

The discontent mounted through 1848 and into the middle of the next year. In August, 1849, Governor

Bennet Riley, who had relieved Colonel Mason in April, realized that further delay would be dangerous. People were even hotly suggesting that California set up her own government as a Pacific Republic independent of the U.S.A. Governor Riley issued a proclamation setting August 1st as the date for an election of municipal officers and convention representatives for the districts of California, all of which he designated. He also chose September 1st as the time for the electorate to assemble at Monterey and begin their business of creating a state.

The hopeful Sutter was the elector chosen to head the Sacramento delegation; with him went Lansford W. Hastings and four others. Peter H. Burnett, Sutter's counsel in all legal matters, was elected chief justice of the Sacramento region on the same day. Up and down the length of California forty-eight men had been selected by ballots cast in camp and town to draw up a constitution.

A new administration had meantime come to Washington with President Zachary Taylor and Vice-President Millard Fillmore. Taylor, the military man, had small patience with Congress's dilatory attitude about California. As far as he was concerned, he hoped that the territory would form its own government and Congress would be literally forced to accept its provisions. Governor Bennet Riley knew Taylor's convictions, which probably hastened his proclamation to enact a civil government.

The convention in Colton Hall at Monterey was a picturesque gathering of notably young men. Six were native Californians. Thomas Larkin, Hugo Reid, Abel Stearns, and John Sutter had been in the province from ten to twenty years. Nearly all the others were Americans. Fourteen were lawyers, Henry W. Halleck and Myron Norton among them; twelve were rancheros; seven were merchants; the remainder were engineers, bankers, and physicians. John McDougall, Joel P. Walker and William M. Gwin, the politician who had purposely come from Washington to become California's first United States Senator, were prominent in discussions. Vallejo, Carrillo, and de la Guerra led the native contingent. Robert Semple was chairman and Edward Gilbert, editor of the *Alta California*, was there to score a clean beat for his paper. Lansford W. Hastings, always willing to be delighted with his own logic, clashed often with the moody-eyed and direct young Irishman, William E. Shannon. One amendment that Shannon introduced was unanimously adopted: "That neither slavery nor involuntary servitude, unless as punishment for crimes, shall ever be tolerated in this state." So California made her own choice on the question, regardless of national opinion or pressure.

A Bill of Rights, formulated on the best points of law already existing in other states, was ratified. The state borders as designated then stand today. San José was chosen as the first capital. A special committee prepared a design for a state seal. Drawn by Major Robert S. Garnett, it is the present Great Seal of California.

On the last day, when the constitution was ready for signing, John Sutter sat as honorary chairman for the event. He set his pen to the document first. The others followed. A salute of thirty-one cannons boomed out to the province that would soon be the thirty-first state in the Union. With the last gun John Sutter leaped upon the rostrum and waved his hands above his head.

"Gentlemen," he cried, "this is the happiest moment of my life. The new state of California has just been born! God grant her honor and eternity!"

A delegation from the convention asked Sutter to be their first governor. He refused. The valley needed him every moment now. He had been absent two months on the business of statemaking. He hurried home.

But his friends put his name on the ballot anyway. Without electioneering of any sort, he ran third in the November election, leading John W. Geary and Winfield S. Sherwood. Peter H. Burnett was elected as the first chief executive of California, leaving Sutter without a clearheaded adviser in business affairs that were now in a puzzling tangle.

Zachary Taylor died on July 9, 1850. By September 9th, Millard Fillmore, his successor, had found enough support to admit California as a state. On October 18th the steamer *Oregon* docked at San Francisco, guns crashing, bunting flying, hoarse voices crying the triumphant news from her decks. Business ceased. Courts adjourned. Newspapers from Washington reporting the admission message sold for $5 each. Cannon roared from the heights. Bonfires blazed when dusk came down. Bands played. Processions came out of nowhere and wound themselves about the town in circles. A celebration spread out over the state that lasted for days as the news journeyed on.

Talk of a Pacific Republic was dead. California had taken her place as another star on America's field of blue. Before the Compromise of 1850 the balance of power between the free states and the slave states had been jealously preserved. Fifteen states of the Union

were free, fifteen slave. The admission of California
with her titanic gold reserves threw the balance of
power to the free states.

The invasion of Sutter's valley went on. In the
first part of 1850 Sutter worked his Indians, plowing
and tilling and sowing. He felt that order and law
would soon make his position secure. "Before the crops
come up we will have better times," he said. So he
labored ceaselessly. The Indians were still decreasing in
numbers. They had been cuffed and beaten and shot
down by the rabble. Many a drunken miner had murdered an Indian for the thrill of hearing him scream.
The natives still worked for the Father of the Fort; but
they ran if strangers came striding down the fields.
More than ever they were hunted things. John Sutter
cursed the gunmen, but it did no good.

Something more came to plague him. Gradually
the new Sacramento City, laid out in lots sold from his
land, took on size and importance. Men no longer came
to the fort to buy. Sacramento stores took away the
trade. One by one the merchants gave up the shops and
storerooms in the great rectangle, once the only commercial center of all interior California. They trans-
ferred their goods to the teeming Sacramento City
streets where wharves, theaters, and gambling houses
lent flavor to frontier life.

By mid-June the change was complete. No storekeeper lived within the adobe walls. All had moved on
to trade where feet stamped loudest. Thieves came by
night to pillage. No monthly gold came to John Sutter
from the rentals.

He left Hock Farm and came to the fort. Some of
the Indians still faithfully tended the garden acres.

Grain was ripening under a golden sun. But the fort was a white ghost looking out on the valley.

To save what he could, John Sutter sold the usable remnants of his stronghold. It was better than letting strangers sack the place. Planks and tools and equipment that remained were carted into Sacramento City. Some were sold at auction, some to private bidders. In the end, his fortress salvage brought him less than $40,000.

Then the crops were ready for harvesting. Only, in a week, the crops ceased to be. Armed men beat down Sutter's harvest for feed; their horses slashed the fields with sharp hoofs, grinding the stalks into the soil. Oxen and sheep were driven in to feed on his grain and grim men with rifles sat beside the trampling herds. Leaden slugs dropped his Indians as they worked.

John Sutter came and saw and raged. He was very close to death in those moments. Then he rode back to Hock. "It can't go on!" he cried savagely. "By Jupiter, it can't go on!"

That winter a quintet of hard-working rascals formed an illicit partnership, with headquarters on an island in the river near Marysville. Armed with rifles and equipped with boats, butcher's tools and helpers, they slaughtered animals and sold meat to Sacramento City inhabitants during the rainy season. Relying on their inaccessible position, they heeded no one. In the spring they divided $60,000 in profits and moved on. Every animal slaughtered had belonged to John Sutter.

Early in 1850 a Squatters Association was formed in San Francisco and Sacramento, its purpose to nullify John Sutter's land claims. Criminals and shyster lawyers were included among some honest men who objected to paying for land without some legal assurance that ownership was clear. They were unsure about Sutter's title and questioned what the final judgment might be. Resolute citizens formed an Anti-Squatters Association to combat the dissatisfied element. Some squatters who moved in and claimed Sacramento City lots were ejected with warnings and guns, if necessary. Dozens died in the grim game.

Land-grabbers were not confined to the Sacramento River region, however. In the Fort Ross and Bodega section they rushed in and squatted on what territory they wanted. William Benitz, Sutter's agent, was as powerless as his chief in the emergency.

The feud between Sacramento City and Sutterville was hot, the stream of trade favoring the Embarcadero town. Buildings rose quickly to serve Sacramento's needs. Lots leaped in price from $500 to $3,000. Hotels were erected. By March, 1850, Sacramento had thirty stores, a printing office, bakery, blacksmith shop, tinshop, billiard room, bowling alley, and six saloons. Hubbard's obscene Round Tent was a popular resort rivaled only by Jim Lee's famous Stinking Tent with its game of monte.

Two more months and profits began to range a hundred per cent higher than the fantastic ones in San Francisco. Rents ran to $5,000 per building a month. Some lots brought $30,000 each. Eight thousand people thronged the gold-mad town.

Choice of irresponsible associates to transact his business in these later moments of stress continued to bring further loss to Sutter. He rushed from agent to agent, fleeced by all. Most of them considered him fair game. No redress was possible. The law had not yet come; only its name. Cunning and might were still in the saddle.

7

In 1850 California was a state without cogs in her political machinery. County government with all its quota of officials was installed slowly and with difficulty. Men were so busy and knew so little about their fellows that rascals were sometimes elected to maintain order. Graft became the rule of the day and justice seemed as far away as before statehood. The tempo of events and the concentrated interest of each man in gold made crime easy. Out of the foothills and the tributary gravel beds of the Sacramento River in 1850 men gathered $41,000,000 in gold. Next year it was $75,000,000; in 1852, $81,000,000. With such riches at stake, honest men let the lawless element run wild, taking time out only occasionally to hang one of the less nimble miscreants caught red-handed in murder or robbery.

For safekeeping, Sutter had filed his three original Mexican grants, the New Helvetia, Sobrante, and "general title" documents, in John S. Fowler's Sacramento law office in 1851. One night someone set fire to the building. In thirty minutes the records were ashes. Rumors began to skip about that Sutter had never actually had such grants anyway.

John McDougall, lately of the constitutional assembly at Monterey, took over Peter Burnett's chair after that reputable official flung up his hands in disgust at the venality about him. The new governor was given to carousals, ruffled white shirt fronts, brass-buttoned blue coats, and frequent unsuccessful attempts at suicide while drunk. He had a keen eye for easy money, also.

He tried to bluff Sutter out of a high-priced block of
Sacramento City lots bordering the Sacramento River,
threatening confiscation and "legal hell-raising." The
bluff didn't work, although Sutter was considerably
angered by the man who feared only two things—"God
and Mrs. John McDougall, sir!"

Anna and the other children reached Hock Farm
during this most crucial phase of Sutter's fight with
suborned politicians and land-hungry pistol jugglers.
It had been seventeen years since he had left them, full
of promises and assured of fortune. Now they found
him engaged in a confused struggle with no quarter
given.

In the last month of 1851, George McKinstry, Jr.,
one of Sutter's "most respectable helpers" in the before-
the-gold era, wrote a letter to Edward Kern in Philadelphia. Kern had been with Frémont during conquest
days and had nominally commanded Sutter's Fort for a
brief time. Wrote McKinstry:

Immediately on the discovery of gold I wrote you and
advised you to hasten out. Yet I presume if you *had* come,
and made the almighty pile, you would have lost it as most
of us have. Since you left this country a most astonishing
change has taken place. The new Yankees would say for the
better, but not we old fellows from Captain Sutter down to
old Bray! The Embarcadero is now the large city of Sacramento. The old fort is rapidly going to decay; the last time
I was there I rode through, and there was not a living thing
to be seen within the walls. Ah, what a fall is there, my
fellow!

The lovely Sacramento, which in our time was only
disturbed by the "well-known, fast-sailing, copper and cop-
per-fastened Clipper-Schooner *Sacramento,* Youckmomney,

Master," is now ploughed day and night from San Francisco to Marysville (old Theodore Cordua's farm) to the Yuba and to Colusa (Larkin's farm) on the Upper Sacramento by most magnificent steamers. These last are generally termed "floating palaces" and are crowded with hungry gold-hunters and speculating Yankees. Times are not what they "useter was."

Due to my long sojourn in the Western Wilds I do not feel at home and I have journeyed down here to San Diego to look at the country. I may purchase a ranch and settle here for life . . . The old Sacramento crowd are much scattered by death and disaster since you left. William Daylor by cholera; Jared Sheldon shot in a row with miners; Perry McCoon by a fall from his horse; Sebastian Keyser drowned; Little Bill Johnson—woeful x—Kin Sabe?; Captain "Luce" missing in the mountains; Olimpio, Sutter's Indian messenger, shot by miners; Old Thomas Hardy, *rum*; John Sinclair, cholera; William E. Shannon, cholera; old William Knight, *rum* as expected; Charley Heath, *rum* and missing; Bob Ridley, fever I think; and others too numerous to set down.

Our good friend Captain John Sutter has fitted up the Hock Rancho in superb style but I regret to say his reign seems smashed to flinders; old Theodore Cordua, tom bien; Daylor and Sheldon estates said to be insolvent; our old and particular crony, John L. Schwartz, still inhabits the Fishing Rancheria and has finally built that two-story house to escape the mosquitoes which he talked about so much. God knows how he stands the present pressure; he goes it, though, more than ever on the rum. Old James McDowell was shot down by miners some two years since—his widow is the owner of Washington, the town opposite Sacramento City; many fine buildings there but at present it is no go—some 500 inhabitants, however.

Old Kitnor is Captain Sutter's mayordomo at Hock— he made a fortune and went bust; William A. Liedesdorff, dead; old Eliab Grimes, dead; Jack Fuller, ditto—also Allen

Montgomery. Montgomery's widow married the man who called himself Talbot H. Green, formerly with Larkin at Monterey and afterwards W. D. M. Howard's partner in San Francisco. His real name was found to be Paul Geddes some time back, a bank robber from the United States. He departed to clear up his character, which was the last seen of him.

Old Louis Keseberg, the Donner Party Man-Eater, has made a fortune and is now running a restaurant on K. street in Sacramento City. I would like to board there, I wouldn't. Pierson B. Reading in on his farm raising wheat and pumpkins in abundance—I camped on his rancho some six weeks last summer. He was the Whig candidate for Governor but could not make it. It was said his friendship with Captain Sutter cost him the Squatter votes. He has been wounded twice in Bear-Hunts since you left—shot in the hand two years ago and broke his leg badly two months ago. Next time it will be his head if he doesn't quit. He plans to go to Philadelphia on the 1st of April next and marry; about time, I think—squaws and niggers won't do. Old Snyder and Sam Hensley both married. Bidwell too damn prosperous to speak of.

Sam Norris has made two or three hundred thousand, but is reputedly hard up and thought to be busted. Sam Brannan, ditto. In fact, I could fill a foolscap sheet with the names of the busted Old Guard in this community, including your humble servant. I purchased the Chico Rancho of old William Dickey, who went to the States or Ireland—I don't know where the hell he is. Old John Yates went to England. Sam Neal is on his farm; he has built a large frame house and still loves horses—still rides the little grey.

Dr. Bates and his brother made a snug fortune—lost it —gone to practicing again. Old Nicolaus Altgeier made a city on his farm. The city blew up and I think the explosion bent him some.

Farming is carried on here to a great extent. Vegetables

raised here would astonish you both as to quantity and size—cabbages 53 pounds per head, Irish potatoes 33 inches in circumference, etc. You ought to visit the country once more "before you die." Short trip by Steamers or by Vera Cruz and Acapulco, which I am told is a very pleasant one; a new line of stages and packs has been established on that route, full as cheap and quick.

Well, I must bring this Dick Sniveler history to a close. I have been writing it down in a room filled with high-strung officers going it loose, full of music and "otard dupy" —some just in from Gila, others from Santa Fé and Colorado . . . I shall expect a long letter from you . . .

Yrs,

George McKinstry, Jr.

The United States Land Commission met in San Francisco for the first time in 1852. They were a federal appointed board to adjudicate the nearly five hundred Mexican grant land titles and confirm or reject each petition as soon as possible. At the end of four years the seven judges had settled three claims. Sutter's was not among them.

Besides this major struggle between the claimants and the federal government, there was continual complicated litigation in progress between individuals over the same tracts. Even when the minor skirmishes had ended, the battle had to be begun again in the Supreme Court of the nation.

To fight with legal weapons costs money. Sutter spent $325,000 in ten years to maintain his title, his occupancy, and to make necessary improvements on his property. For twenty years the federal government was credited with robbing seven of every eight claimants seeking justice before the United States Land Commission, making the private citizen, at prohibitive expense, defend his title against powerful opposition that had no costs to pay. The very people who had been assured of their land titles by the Treaty of Guadalupe Hidalgo, following the Mexican War, were thus despoiled. It was probably the most flagrant government confiscation of property in modern times, if we except the land-grabbing of totalitarian states. The uncertainty of landownership held in check the development of the state's natural resources for two decades.

From the tented town of 1849, San Francisco had become a well-built city by the summer of 1852, boasting all the activities and physical equipment necessary to a metropolis. Art, religion, the theater, newspapers, trade, and the Stock Exchange kept pace with scandal, graft, politics, gambling houses, and the courts. Canvas stretched over scantling had given way to wood and stone, brick and marble and iron as building material. Fire had razed the town six times in eighteen months at a cost of $30,000,000. But carpenters were at work in the hot ashes after each catastrophe. There was a use now for huge mirrors, rich draperies, vintage wines, and imported foods. "Magnificent accommodations" could be had by those who had found gold or taken it away from somebody else. There were thumping music and glaring chandeliers and Brussels carpets and "dens of loathsome vice." The Fire Department was a collection of clubs quartered in imposing firehouses in different sections, equipped with shining engines of the "latest extraordinary scientific design" and distinctive uniforms. They staged races to conflagrations, colliding often with rival engines in their haste. If one company arrived first and took the best place from which to "throw water," the tardy crews were always willing to join in a free-for-all, clubbing with hose nozzles and speaking trumpets, spectators not barred. Mascots, ranging from dogs to half-wits, were hurried along with each engine charging to the flames.

Nathaniel Currier, of Currier and Ives, had just made lithograph tabloids available to the American public and any spectacular event in San Francisco was thus distributed through Currier's pictorial medium. Newspapers were as numerous as dogfights.

Every man dressed to his own taste. Miners gambled in red flannel shirts, battered broad hats, "stagged" trousers, boots, and the wide pistol belts of the digger. You could see men in tall white hats, frilled shirts, brass-buttoned blue tail coats, varnished boots, with perhaps even a gold-headed Malacca cane carried in a gloved hand. The stores carried every necessity "for the elegantly dressed man" that could be found in a London shop.

Each nationality had its home section about the city, its favorite eating places, a band of its own, and celebrated its native holiday. The arrival of a ship was a social event and constituted important news for days. Parades were never out of place and everybody, including the Fire Department, always turned out with torches and enthusiasm to turn the most modest occasion into a good show.

The citizens, on two occasions, had to form Committees of Vigilance against criminals. Too often the courts proved themselves convenient instruments for legalizing injustice. So San Franciscans, stung to action by particularly brutal murders and thefts, abruptly hanged a number of culprits after a fair public trial.

For a time, the medicine was efficient; at least it gave pause to hardened criminals of the Australian "Sydney Duck" and Chileno type who had slight stomach for decorating a rope-end.

The city had gaiety and charm and a unique personality, despite dust, sea winds, graft, and sudden death. The tempo of the town was fast. Everyone was always in a hurry. Silver-mounted hacks and "gentlemen's elegant private equipages" with gold-handled whips snapping above smart teams were the only highway carriers that could be called dignified. The noise of the rabble was comparable to a "hogshead full of cats" in midnight holiday. The town was crowded with newsboys, children with firecrackers, merchants, horsemen galloping over plank toll roads, Hindus, pig-tailed Chinese, bankers, Russians, cigar boys crying their wares, women struggling with parasols, actors bursting with "city and inland engagements," Turks, Kanakas, bootblacks cracking dirty rags, mules, horses, and swaggering Mexicans. Living was a breathless business and everybody's schemes were sure to pan out.

The river and the valley changed with San Francisco. Sacramento City made itself into the state capital. The stronger valley towns destroyed the weaker ones with economic pressure. The wilderness of the days of Spanish and Mexican occupation was crisscrossed now with beaten roads and dotted with garden patches and fields of growing things. The river was a great highway. Homes were no longer so far apart that it was comforting to see the smoke from your neighbor's chimney. Gold still directed river and valley growth, and continued to do so until Civil War days. But men were daily more concerned with the land and crops that could be sold.

Surprisingly, in 1857, the Land Commission decided in John Sutter's favor. Rejoicing came to Hock Farm. The squatters were furious. They appealed to the United States District Court of Northern California. In 1858 a decision was made that "these grants are perfect and legal in all respects." The squatters carried the fight to the Supreme Court of the United States. Then came the final word: the New Helvetia grant was confirmed; the Sobrante and "general title" grants were declared invalid. The highest tribunal admitted his grants "just and meritorious." In reviewing the case, the attorney general's argument was almost naïve: "It is against the public policy," he declaimed, "for one man to hold the fee of so much land."

Sutter contended the statement didn't make sense. Either all his grants were legal, or none. He had given titles to much of the Sobrante grant under deeds of personal warranty. After the adverse decision, he was forced to make good these deeds from his confirmed New Helvetia grant. In reality, the legalization of the one grant availed him little. Even Hock Farm began to be eaten up by debt and lawyer's fees and attachment. Fort Ross land was also lost to him by clouded title.

In 1865 Hock Farm was fired in the night and burned to the ground. The vandals were only a few hours ahead of legal action to dispossess John Sutter and Anna. The children were married and gone. Resolutely, Sutter turned his face east, swore to go to Washington and demand justice of Congress. When he left California he was sixty-six years old, slower, grayer, and rheumatism was in his bones from trail days. But he was still sure of himself. He settled in Lititz, in Lancaster County, Pennsylvania, and began to make periodic trips to Washington.

Congress delayed action interminably in his case. More years sped by. He hoped, finally, for only $50,000 —a gesture of payment for the Sobrante grant. He died, one hot June day in 1880, in a little hotel room in America's Capital City, just as his friend General William Tecumseh Sherman brought him news that Congress had once more shelved his petition.

8

Near Marysville, early in 1852, a preacher's son and a carpenter were starting a war. Their weapons were shovels, saws, hammers, wooden boxing, and a roll of stout sailcloth. They had dug a ditch that held running water and beyond that they had set in a hundred feet of wooden boxing to bring the ditchwater close to a bank of golden gravel. The water was checked by endgates as they worked. The sailcloth had been made into a crude hose and fitted, none too snugly, over the end of the pine boxing. Then the water rushed through their wooden housing into the tapering canvas hose. Out gushed the torrent with a roar. Cautiously they played the stream back and forth over the rich gravel. It began to blast away the bank and carry the earth into the sluice boxes they had built below. There the quicksilvered riffles caught the heavy gold from the muddy current, holding the treasure until the time when the water could be shut off and the amalgam gathered.

Joe Wood, the preacher's son from Ohio, and John

Payne, the carpenter from Maine, shouted congratulations to each other over the hose-end as they swept it from side to side. They had found an easy way to mine gold! They had no thought that they had begun the bitterest mining war in California's history, that they had fired the first gun of a forty-year conflict. Out of their tiny rush of water grew a flood of saffron muck—"slickens"—that carried a devastating mass of sand and gravel over doomed farm lands once radiantly fruitful. The muck crept into the Feather and Bear and Yuba and American to build up channel beds until no boats larger than launches could use the streams and until fish no longer lived in the polluted waters. It swirled on into the Sacramento, driving the great steamers from the river, bringing floods in the rainy season that spread destruction to rich valley crops and city streets alike.

Joe Wood and John Payne were ingenious beginners. Edward Mathewson, a Connecticut Yankee, followed their lead in Nevada County. Soon they had a hundred imitators with ideas. Iron pipe took the place of wooden boxing. For a time sturdy sailcloth continued duty as the nozzle. Then, in swift succession, came "Craig's Globe Monitor," "Fisher's Knuckle Joint," and "Hoskin's Improved Nozzle," all the devices of "practical miners." These iron nozzles supplanted the canvas kind and threw water under terrific pressure upon the banks of golden gravel. The machines, called "monitors," were more pliant than the old type; they could be moved in any direction with ease and little effort. The area that no one yet recognized as a battlefield spread out, as fast as men could find water and dig ditches near gold-bearing banks. Now the "Little Giants"—affectionately named by the men who worked them—began to throw a thousand or more miner's inches of water each. A whole battery could play along the same bank and their voices were as loud as their bite was strong.

"Big Ben" Brady, playing his monitor on the Blue Gravel banks at Sucker's Flat, would yowl soundlessly into the roar about him, sure that he was washing more gravel than "Rainbow Pete" Marr and his "Piffling Puddler" on Indiana Hill at Gold Run. Rainbow Pete was above comparing his artistic handling of a Little Giant with a low-life nobody in the mining fraternity like Big Ben. But Pete was pretty mad at "that English dude wearin' topmast stunsail collars just like a broker," an office clerk of the London-owned Gold Run Hydraulic Mining Company, who had christened Pete's proud monitor the "Piffling Puddler."

The new kind of mining started legends of prowess in the land and for the three decades that California's huge monitors washed ten millions in gold each year the tales grew folklike and persistent. Today, with hydraulic mining officially dead this half century in all except one isolated Trinity region, the old stories are still told where old men foregather in old towns whose names are almost forgotten, out-of-the-way clumps of ramshackle buildings deep in California's hills. Hank Small makes his mighty stand beside his Little Giant, blasting a falling wall of gravel into sky-drift as his mates escape, plays the nozzle as the enveloping wall creeps in upon him from behind like a resistless shroud. Jake Herrold and his mad mule, Molly, "fly through the air with the greatest of ease," victims of the Dead Fish monitor at Dutch Flat, and it is stoutly claimed by men who know that Jake and Molly never came back to earth, so great was the power of the monitor that lifted them. The walls cave in on Custis James and his sweetheart, Ellen Gray, on that day she came for the first and last time to see her lover swing a Little Giant near Big Meadows. "One-Arm Andy" Klotz hoists his monitor on his back and carries it home every night where, shined by red flannel and bear's grease it sleeps under his bunk, covered by a clean tarpaulin.

And "Galloping Jack" Malloy and his terrier, Tom, search among ten thousand kegs in the powder house of the Blue Gravel Mine, candle held high for a black cat that was never found. Nor, for that matter, were Galloping Jack and Tom.

Some of the golden banks stood up under the attack of Little Giants. The Blue Gravel Hydraulic Mine at Sucker's Flat in Yuba County consisted of acre after acre of auriferous gravel mixed with sand and clay, a combination that bound the mass together into a conglomerate so hard that the monitors could not break it down. In 1869 twelve hundred kegs of powder were blasted at one time to loosen the gravel for the monitors.

The mine was throwing five million gallons of water a day, at a pressure of 150 feet. Already the Blue Gravel had produced $1,300,000 and the yield was swiftly mounting.

Foreign capital came to California in steadily increasing amounts. The Gold Run Hydraulic Mining Company was owned by a London firm. In Plumas County the Hungarian Mining Company controlled extensive fields. A French corporation was interested in Yuba County holdings and an Australian company mined near by. Although American owners were predominant, some of the richest individual mines were foreign owned and operated.

By the beginning of the seventies the hundreds of original small claims in the Marysville region had been taken over by six big firms working with "Little Giants and giant powder." No time was wasted. The companies demanded quick returns. If the monitors met cementlike resistance, a tunnel was run, drifts cut, powder kegs rolled in, and a blast set off. Then the monitors took up the task and made sluice fodder of the blasted banks. On June 9, 1871, on a claim near Smartsville in Yuba County, two thousand kegs of powder raised 150,000 cubic yards of gravel ten feet so that the Little Giants could slide the golden mass through the sluiceways. In two more years the nozzles became so improved that it was no longer necessary to blast.

In the spring of 1873 the Hungarian Mining Company was just getting into stride at Quigley's Ravine, in Plumas County. It laid out thousands of feet of huge iron pipe, built large flumes, constructed reservoirs, and dug miles of ditch. There was an 1,800-foot flume, in four sections. It was four feet eight inches wide and carried a thousand inches of water on a six-inch grade. Two large "undercurrents" caught all the gold. There was no waste. Between the four sections of flume were ground sluices designed to break up the dirt lest it pass off in "chunks." Quigley's Ravine gravel ran two hundred feet deep and contained gold from surface to bed-rock. A passing mining engineer was moved to wonder as he saw two huge Little Giants crashing a thousand inches of water each at the bank. With three hundred feet of pressure shooting out of the nozzles, the flume was kept running constantly at capacity and the banks were tossed away like sea-drift in a gale. Rocks weighing hundreds of pounds were bounced about the flume like runaway pebbles and finally came to rest in the canyon below. "It was a rather impressive display," wrote the engineer, "as to what man will do to change the face of the earth, swiftly and fiercely, for the treasure hidden in it."

The Dutch Flat Blue Gravel Company had also installed improved monitors, as had the Little York Hydraulic Company in the same region. Over in Oroville, nearly a thousand Chinese were arriving by train or stage each month for the new diggings below. At least two astute Chinese owned and operated hydraulic mines there and employed their countrymen exclusively. The North Fork Mining Company of Plumas County had completed a tremendous hydraulic development in 1874 with more than twenty-five miles of difficult ditchwork and eight miles of pipe. The mines lay near the North Fork of the Feather, six miles south of Big Meadows, and the use of Rice's Creek was included in the water privileges of the company. Ah Shune, of Silver Creek, was the most important contractor employed by the North Fork Mining Company promoters and he built six miles of flume for them on the Butte Valley ridge. His six-foot wide, yard-deep flume was the best-built section of their holdings and yellow hands made every foot of it.

Hydraulic mining had begun in the Gold Run and Dutch Flat regions in '65. Gold Run was developed by the Indiana Hill Cement Mining Company and the Gold Run Hydraulic Company. The two factions were never notably friendly and many English chins were hit by Irish fists during the disputes. The Dutch Flat hydraulic mines were extensive. The Franklin, Harkness, Cedar Creek, and San Francisco tunnel companies held large gravel concessions. So did the Dead Fish and Golden Calf mines, Huysink's, and Raymond and Doolittle's.

All the great hydraulic firms were in a continual pother about water rights. They owned lakes and made lakes in the Sierras, bickering as much among themselves as with the farmers and townsfolk below who hated the murky tide of debris sloshing endlessly into the valleys. Each year the discharge of muck was growing. On Cherokee Flat the Spring Valley Mining and Irrigation Company was feeding its Little Giants 36,000,000 gallons of water daily in the summer. In spring they doubled that flow. And they were but one mine of many.

Richness in one golden crop meant poverty in another. In the late fifties hydraulic mining had first begun to damage the orchards and wheatlands of the Yuba and Feather, the Bear and the American. Resentment and turmoil heightened as the debris rolled on to the Sacramento and the valley. "When sand and small

stones and slickens hits the land we're all through,"
moaned the farmers. With faces grim and patience
gone, they formed the Anti-Debris Association of the
Sacramento Valley to fight the masters of the Little
Giants. Hundreds joined them: Tom Brophy of Sutter
County, Jasper of Yuba, Jonas Marcuse, Eli Davis,
Wilson, Wilbur, and Chandler who chewed dollar Ha-
vanas into shreds in the stress of speechmaking. The
Bear River region sent Dr. Durst, Haile, Armstead,
Dresher, Huff, and Wood. Senator Pardee, Chris Green,
Joe Routier, Camron, and Carey led the farmers' fight
and gave financial help. The state appointed a Mining
Debris Assembly in 1878 to survey the damage already
done. Reuben Kercheval was a member and he was
dismayed by the sight of wastelands by the rivers where
orchards and gardens and golden wheatfields had been.
"Small fruit boats scrape their bottoms now," he told
the Assembly acidly, "where great steamers I saw in
the fifties ran by with depth to spare." Yuba City had
begun a vanguard battle against hydraulic mining three
years earlier and their Citizens' Committee slapped affi-
davits on the State Assembly table until the members
were dizzied by the number of them.

Mayor C. E. Stone of Marysville added his word to
the mounting fight-talk. He remembered his arrival at
Marysville in 1850 when ships were moored in the clear,
fish-filled, thirty-foot water of the Yuba as far as the
vanished town of Eliza five miles below the city. Now
the fish were gone and the steamers were replaced by
rowboats. The bed of the Yuba was so filled with debris
that the river was almost level with Marysville streets
and the levees were overflowed each year. Mayor Stone
predicted utter ruin when the new hydraulic mine near

Oroville and Quincy began to run at capacity into the Feather. He talked of the acres upon the Feather and Yuba, once green and fruitful and dotted with prosperous homes, now covered with a sticky compound of clay and sand, topped by pebbles. He recalled the Briggs Orchard near Marysville, once sold for a quarter of a million dollars, now covered with debris twenty feet deep. And the one-time prosperous ranch of the Grass Brothers, for which they paid $300 an acre, lay in the grip of the silt.

"The miners," said Stone, "claim the right to dump into our rivers because the United States government sold them the mining ground, with the right to work it. We claim the right to the free and unhindered possession of our homes and lands and the use of our rivers because the United States government, by solemn treaty, has guaranteed to these holdings under Mexican grants all the rights acquired under that government. Gentlemen—" and Stone struck his fist sharply on the Assembly table— "no miner has been allowed to throw the tailings of his mine on the one below it since the first discovery of gold in California. Is it justice to start it now? Every day hydraulic miners work their claims they are violating treaty rights granted our lands through Mexican grants!"

Stone was a gloomy and determined person. But he was not so desperate as the men and women whose homes and lands lay engulfed by the hydraulic drift.

A climax came in the famous test case of *James H. Keyes* v. *Little York Mining Company*, and a dozen other hydraulic mines and their owners. Excitement ran high for weeks and months. The case was won by Keyes and was as promptly appealed to the higher courts by the miners. The state was blazing with surmise and threats. There were tales of bribery and corruption, of intimidated witnesses, of "big money" paid by the hydraulickers to people "higher up." Men read the newspapers and congregated at telegraph office newsboards. The defense presented engineering experts and used every conceivable device to prove the innocence of the Little Giants. But Keyes was stubbornly unshaken in his testimony, although constantly baited and derided by the opposing counsel. Charley Justis came down from Wheatland as a witness to bolster Keyes's evidence. Justis told ugly stories of once rich orchards and fields on Bear River. Pat Carroll came forward with his story of disaster. D. A. Ostrom testified to the devastation of the land on Dry Creek. W. H. Drum was there from Yuba River to tell of his home with slickens running over the eaves. "I built it when we were twenty-three feet above high-water mark," he said.

Jim Keyes won again in the higher tribunals. The news gave hope to half a million persons. Judge Sawyer's decision in the United States Circuit Court in 1884 was but the first of a flood of injunctions against the Little Giants. One by one they were silenced and soon even the echo of their voices was gone. Farmers breathed more easily and walked with more assurance. Never again, they felt, would the yellow muck come down the rivers.

Men spoke of the past as if it had been an evil dream. In one year alone 46 million cubic yards of gravel, a mass a mile wide and a mile long and fifteen yards deep, had been hurled into the streams or spread over the farm lands. Hydraulic mining on such a scale had never been attempted in the world before. In thirty years two billion cubic yards of slickens silted the tributaries of the Sacramento and the great river itself.

Federal legislation created the California Debris Commission Act in 1893, perhaps the final curtain for the Little Giants. The discharge of debris into the rivers was declared illegal forever.

But today's engineers claim that the erection of three dams at strategic points would impound all debris in certain sections on the Bear, American, and Yuba rivers; that hydraulic mining could be resumed legally and actually keep natural debris from going downstream and silting the Sacramento channel. There still remain in this region the largest gold-bearing gravel deposits known to the mining world and the only process by which they can be worked is hydraulic mining. Under the new conditions some 800 million cubic yards of treasure-laden banks await the Little Giants. It is estimated that it would take forty years to mine this gravel still hiding its gold in the California earth.

9

One June morning in 1849, Reuben Kercheval, lean of hip and wide of shoulder, sat on a boulder by Moccasin Creek, thinking. He had mined for two hours and had four bits' worth of gold to show for it. Near him a score of miners toiled at their backbreaking task in the creek bed. An idea had burst on him as he bent over his rocker. Its common-sense values grew as he sat on the boulder. Miners had to eat. There were thousands of them. More were coming. And California vegetable prices made a farmer feel like a banker. Flour was a dollar a pound.

THE 1850's IN
SACRAMENTO
CITY

Reuben Kercheval rose from his rock, slung his shovel through his pack-straps, hawked the rest of his miner's outfit by boulder auction and set out briskly for Sacramento's busy streets. Four days later he and his shovel were in a secondhand rowboat on their way down the Sacramento.

His uncle, Armstead Runyon, was just beginning to try his luck at farming near the site of modern Courtland. Reuben joined him because he wanted to be near Sacramento City. A man could fill his rowboat with fruit and vegetables and reach a clamoring market swiftly if he did not have to row upstream too far. So Kercheval and Runyon and Jim Collins and Bill Holltum and a half dozen others took over what is now the incomparably fruitful Grand Island, then only a rich swampland sitting perilously low beside the sparkling river.

As Kercheval worked in vegetable patches and dug holes for young fruit trees he was thinking about levees. He tried to interest his friends, but they were too busy digging and planting to be concerned about dikes to hold the river away from the lands. It hadn't happened yet. Meet a thing when it came, they said. In fact, they found their fellow "swamplander" a little tiresome. Kercheval was always stubborn when he was sure of what he was talking about. So he began to portion out his time and pile up a low levee near the head of Steamboat Slough on the riverbank fronting his land.

Up in Sacramento City the council, prodded by Sam Brannan, followed Kercheval's lead. "Man named Kercheval down by the Slough has the right idea," said Brannan. "Let's not wait until the river rolls in on us; let us guarantee our security now." Late in 1850 a levee a yard high, six feet wide at the crest and four yards across the base was built by the city. It began on high ground near Sutterville, ran west to the east bank of the Sacramento and then north to the mouth of the American. From there it wandered nearly three miles along the south bank of the American and east to high ground. The city fathers were quite proud of it.

Kercheval and his neighbors were lucky farmers in 1850. More so the next year, even if prices were not so high, because the state took over a million and three-quarters acres of swamplands by grant from the federal government. Plans were being made for reclamation and sale of much of it. The Reclamation Commission immediately endeared itself to Kercheval and his clan by giving 640 acres on Merritt Island outright to Dave

Calloway and Jack Booth, newcomers to the river, provided they build levees and cultivate the land as an experiment. The indignant snorts from Grand Island bothered the politicians for a time. No further grants were made, even to brothers of politicians.

Kercheval piled his levees higher in 1851 while Sutter sat bewildered at Hock Farm, most of his empire given over to squatters. The Grand Island farmers paid no attention to squatter riots. They had troubles of their own. They had a foothold in the lush land and no time to meddle in squabbles.

The river came roaring down and swept the Sacramento levees toward San Francisco Bay in the next spring, and took Kercheval's tiny dikes along with them. All the swamplands sank under a turbid inland sea and from Sacramento City to the river's mouth the farmers slept in rowboats, treetops, and on high ground. His neighbors vowed to listen to Reuben Kercheval thereafter. His fight for levees had never ceased and now his arguments were backed up by floodwaters. The floods went away and Reuben Kercheval married a lighthearted, "raven-haired lass from the East" and built a costly frame house on the island. But he did not let his neighbors forget their high-water promises. It was rough going and they were almost as mulish as ever. Now and again he lost his temper, but his opposition was never able to escape from him.

"We have to fight the river together," was his line of attack. "No man can do it alone. And we can't afford to put it off till high water!"

He built twelve miles of levee on the upper end of Grand Island. Chinese and Indians and Kanakas swung shovels and trundled wheelbarrows to fill in the thirteen-foot base of the levee and angle off its yard-high, yard-wide crest. That twelve miles was built entirely at Reuben Kercheval's expense. The dirt was taken from the land side of the levee because there was no way to scoop sand out of the river. Foremen of the levee gangs walked the crest ceaselessly, revolvers in their belts, alert to prevent the Chinese from throwing stumps into their wheelbarrows to fatten the 13½-cent wage they received for every cubic yard moved.

Back of his barriers Kercheval was still planting fruit trees, setting out grapevines, putting more acres under cultivation, still talking levees. During the three or four years after 1853 he was able to force his neighbors to build small dikes of their own along the Grand Island line of the river. These levees joined in a continuous wall along the banks of Old River and Steamboat Slough. In this way, as Kercheval put it, the levees "jest growed" for eighteen miles until they enclosed the upper island entirely. The lower end was unfortunately left open. The levees were built by individual owners whose tastes were as uniform as a Sierra sky line. "You can tell," Kercheval often said plainly, "just how stingy or generous a man is by the height of his levee and the width of his base line."

A law was passed in 1855 allowing the swamplands to be taken up in 320-acre tracts at $1 an acre. The swamplanders breathed easier after that. Some of Kercheval's neighbors had objected to building levees until assured of their land titles. Now that objection was gone. Four years later amendments made it possible for a man to own 640 acres.

Other island farmers began serious levee building. Andrus, Brannan, Sherman, and some men on Merritt

Island began to put gangs of Chinese and Indians and Kanakas to work along their river banks. Kercheval's sons grew large enough to play under fruit trees and set toy boats in the river. He had grain and pears and peaches and corn and beans and potatoes and cabbages to send up and down the river now, carried mostly in his own light-draught schooner. The land was good to Reuben Kercheval but he still talked of higher levees.

In 1861 the dikes of Grand Island were crashed aside like a line of paper barriers. The swamplands became a sea again. Fruit trees and grape arbors were uprooted and vegetable furrows erased. The waters swirled over the buildings and carried them away.

Kercheval kept on demanding levees. They were rebuilt grudgingly and strengthened. They withstood the waters until the flood of 1868. After those desperate days, Kercheval hurried repairs and this time he built almost high and strong enough to satisfy himself. His levees were forty feet at the base, eight feet high and a yard across at the crest. He still muttered at his neighbors, however. They persisted in building dikes as they pleased and simply grinned when Kercheval pointed out wearily that the levees were only as strong as their weakest banks. That same year a law was passed slashing all acreage restrictions from state swamplands. Men scrambled to buy a million acres. One gambler in futures bought 98,120 acres—153 square miles. The era of the capitalist had arrived and most of the small landholders were against this concentration of land in a few hands.

Soon Kercheval went to work on a reclamation project for Grand Island. He wanted powers to build levees and assess the island property to pay for them.

A special act of the legislature finally ratified the bill. By the early seventies, under Kercheval's direction, $110,000 was collected "for the uniform protection of our island." That very year the river rose again and Kercheval's levees on the Steamboat Slough frontage caved in. Half the island acreage was covered once more.

Then Reuben Kercheval passed a bright milestone. Grand Island's 17,000 fertile acres stood entirely surrounded by a uniform levee! A man could pace 29½ circuitous miles and return to his starting place without stepping from the dikes. He felt safe now. So did his island clan. They held a "Levee Day" to prove it and made speeches and ate only what the island produced, "a dinner fit for the gods."

But now Kercheval was plagued with the debris of hydraulic mining that threatened his dikes anew. Each year he had watched the swirling, sand-clouded waters build up the river bed. Each year the levees had to go higher to match the rise in the channel level. Each year, with countless others, he had hoped the debris menace would grow less acute. But it only bulked larger.

Nevertheless, the next few years were untroubled, productive times for the men of Grand Island. General Thomas H. Williams spent thousands in putting his acreage under cultivation and his grainfields were ten times the size of Kercheval's holdings. In Yolo, back of Clarksburg, Williams owned another 20,000 acres and in public opinion he was a land-hog. People disliked him because he hired Chinese in preference to white labor. The general retorted that enough whites were never available when his crops needed them. He added that Kercheval used twice as many Chinese for levee work as he did.

The great dikes of Grand Island fell before the rains and the river in the spring of 1876. The crops were reaped by the winds and waters and Kercheval swore, once and for all, to build levees that no river would top. That fall he raised $156,000 and went to work with 200 Chinese and 40 Kanakas. At strategic points he made the base of the dike 100 feet thick, 12 feet high, with a 5-foot crest. He ordered all the fill material to be carried across the levee from the river side and dumped inside. Then he had the Chinese drive a double row of stakes on the line of the levee and pad this in with sacks of dirt and sand and debris. When he had finished, in the low-water, big-crop year of 1877, he was sure the river was beaten. Even the "Grand Island Grouch," J. W. Brocas, smiled when he looked at Kercheval's latest work. The leveemaker was elected assemblyman for Sacramento County and he promised that he would persuade everyone along the river to build waterproof dikes as did the wise men of Grand Island.

But the early spring rains of the following year were ceaseless and the river high. A levee break at Mill's ranch below Freeport was caught in time. It was blamed on the hole-digging gophers and poison was set for them. Kercheval was at Sacramento City when news came of a dike weakness at Grand Island. He and C. W. Clarke went down on the *Whipple* on February 8th. Under the driving of Kercheval's familiar voice the gang of Chinese buttressed the break. Next day Kercheval sent a dispatch to Sacramento: "The levee is all

right, the washout is under control, and the island is
looking fine."

Then the Sutterville levee gave way. While the city
council debated what to do, the townsfolk of Sacramento made a holiday of the affair. Seven young blades
of the Undine Boat Club took the "club barge through
the levee break like the wind," their colors flying at the
stern, their voices raised in cheers as they flashed by on
the murky flood. A snag caught them amidships,
snapped off their rudder, and dumped them all into a
mud bank. "Seven Ethiopians carried the barge back
along the levee to the boathouse."

Across the river, on the Washington side, the citizens guarded their dikes all that night with a shotgun
patrol. A rumor had reached them that an attempt
would be made to dynamite the levee to relieve the
pressure on the Sacramento City side.

Suddenly the levee went in at Freeport and the
country below frothed into a shallow lake. Kercheval
made another inspection of Grand Island that same
day, before returning to Sacramento. He felt that the
levee would stand a further rise of three or four feet
without danger. He particularly watched the wing dam
on Old River, because there the current formed strong
eddies that cut voraciously into the bank. The main
levee, he reported, had not even been touched by the
water. But the old embankment outside showed signs
of giving way and he set his Chinese and Kanakas to
bank the curve all along the danger spot with earth,
rocks, brush, and bales of hay. Every islander felt rea-
sonably secure and plows were turning up the land
every day as the river rose. General Williams ordered
the steamer *Enterprise* to tow the pile driver from

Three Mile Slough to the wing dam where a number of piles had been undermined by the current.

That night the river and the valley were whipped by gale winds and drenched under torrents of rain. In the morning State Senator William Johnston of Richland and Sol Runyon of Onisbo reached Sacramento with news that the floods had reached the Pierson levee below Dwight Hollister's ranch, but the levee was still holding. The tornado intensity of the storm held all night.

The gale even sharpened its fury on February 14th. The *Enterprise*, with its pile driver and barge loaded with piles, was blown ashore at Collinsville. Captain Foster of the *Julia* left Sacramento at once to get her off. The Pierson levee continued to hold but on the inside of the "Pocket" from Sacramento City to Randall Island the water was up to the base of the low dikes. At Freeport, ten-year-old Rocky Hunt, whose boyhood has a place in this river story, was gleefully watching the waters rolling over the toprail of the schoolhouse fence and planning with his brothers to take their rowboat out on the flooded Sacramento River and look for "treasure drift."

A group of men were laying plans for a 45-mile canal to aid the river runoff. It was to begin six miles above the mouth of Feather River and finally empty into Suisun Bay. Wm. P. Coleman, Mike Bryte, Chris Green, and Albert Gallatin were all for the idea. So were Linnell and Harkness and Hamilton and Captain Bill Blanding. A meeting was called in Fireman's Hall on the fifteenth and the canal project debated. Kercheval opposed it; he wanted higher and stronger dikes. Assemblyman Dare of Solano thought it was fighting the Almighty, and shrilled that the whole thing was being done in the interest of the swampland owners. Sargent of San Joaquin County favored the canal. Even the pressure of the gale outside did not bring unanimity to Fireman's Hall.

Four inches of rain fell in four hours on February 18th. A levee break came at Deadman's Drift on the Griffin ranch, six miles below Washington near Riverside Ferry. The water had filled the tule lands back of the break and was crashing against Gwynn's new levee opposite Freeport. This flood cut at the inner side of the dike as the river battered it from the stream side. Waves going over the levee carried a dozen courageous sandbaggers to their death. Working against time, Bill Gwynn sent a steamer down, carrying 35,000 feet of lumber, 5,000 sacks, and 50 men in a last effort to save the walls.

Next morning Captain Fairfield of the *Centennial* brought unsettling news to Sacramento. At daylight he had passed a new break on the Yolo side below Five Mile House at Williams's ranch. A fierce torrent crashing into the tule lands beyond had contemptuously up-ended Williams's house and barn and hurled them a quarter mile away.

This new rush of water backed its way up against the Gwynn dike, adding to the pressure on it. The levee went out with a roar and the reclaimed Lisbon district became an ocean. Back of Walnut Grove the country was underwater, flooded by the Mokelumne and Cosumnes rivers.

Bad reports came by steamer up the river. The water was higher in Steamboat Slough and Old River than at any time since levees had surrounded the island, but not so high as the floods of 1862. The dikes were still holding well but it was feared that they would go out when the torrent pouring through the Williams's ranch break swirled into Cache Creek Slough and Steamboat Slough below the Hog's Back.

The Sacramento rose to 25 feet 10 inches, higher than ever before, on the twentieth. The levee below Washington on the Yolo side broke and boats were busy rescuing the inhabitants and ferrying them across to Sacramento. When the steamer *Cora* passed Sherman Island in the lower river the entire island was submerged. The levee had given way below Emmaton and the water was still rising. The levees around Andrus, Brannan, and Staten islands were overflowed. "Grand Island—hurrah for Kercheval!—is still all right and expected to hold." The Pierson levee had met disaster and so had the Clarke levee. All the country from Sacramento to Collinsville was underwater except Grand Island.

All that night a gale lashed the river and the underwater valley. Rains fell without pause. Next morning the river threw its final attack at Kercheval's levees. At Lovedall's, on Steamboat Slough, a short space below the Hog's Back, the dikes had settled two feet lower than elsewhere on the island. At noon, on the deck of a steamer racing down the river, Reuben Kercheval was just in time to see the murky waters top the Lovedall levee. The break widened three hundred feet before his unbelieving eyes. An hour later the island was a storm-lashed lake. The last reclaimed land in the valley had bowed to the river.

There were nightmare days and nights for a week thereafter. Cattle stood in water on the remaining levee banks or were swept away. Orchards were treetops bobbing in water. Steamers, careful of snags, fought their way up and down the river with refugees. Masses of driftwood piled up on high ground or broke fruit trees into the debris-choked waters. A hundred people were drowned. Buildings whirled downstream or withstood the flood with only their roofs above the current. Kercheval's Grand Island Chinese, burdened with packs and splattered with mud, scrambled up and down the levees, screaming at the passing boats to take them off.

The entire lowlands of the Sacramento Valley were flooded as far as Suisun Bay. Only Sacramento City and a few towns protected by levees escaped. Losses were in the millions. Kercheval and General Williams sent Captain Foster with the *Chin-du-Wan* and barges down to Grand Island to rescue their stock. His family beside him, Kercheval sailed over the island in his schooner. Nothing showed abovewater on Grand Island except the hotel and the dock. Ah Jack, Kercheval's Chinese contractor, was missing with $6,000 belonging to his Chinese laborers, who had entrusted him with sums ranging from $20 to $200 each. Ah Jack's countrymen had this calamity added to their troubles. General Tom Williams said that they were the hottest coolies he had ever seen bemoaning cold cash. The lost Ah Jack is still lost. And no one knows whether, true to his trust, he met death in the wild waters or whether he saved his life and absconded with the $6,000.

Kercheval brought his family to Sacramento City on the *Whipple* to await the end of the floodtime. For nearly twenty years he had fought the river with levees. He still felt levees were the answer. "It's not the river, gentlemen," he said bluntly at a State Assembly meeting in March. "It's the debris spewed into the rivers that makes our levees forever too low to hold the floods in check. Stop hydraulic mining and our levees will hold!"

He sat down in a stormy chorus of boos and cheers.

When the waters went down, the men of Grand Island returned to their land. Kercheval imposed new tax levies and set about raising the dikes to a new high. New fruit trees were put out and remaining old ones propped upright and rerooted. Planting went on. Plows furrowed the fields. Houses and barns were rebuilt or scraped out and repainted.

Then in February of 1881 the river went mad again, prodded by the huge hydraulic monitors. The Sacramento *Bee*, edited for eighty years by the Mc-Clatchys, father and son, two of the greatest newspaper personalities in the West, called the river "our Murmuring Brook" and staged a brave show of deprecating the disaster. But once more the reclaimed lands went underwater from Sacramento City to Collinsville.

Kercheval refused to be interviewed about the flood by a Sacramento *Bee* reporter. But Mike Bryte, "the tallest man in the Sacramento Valley," was willing. He was smiling and undisturbed, even though his dairy ranch above Washington was almost entirely underwater.

"How do you and your men manage to live in these perilous times?" asked the newsman.

"Oh, we do fairly well," said Mike casually. "In the morning we look out of the second story to see if any of the valley is still in sight. If it is, I go downstairs and take soundings in the cooking stove. If it's full of water I call down the boys and we set to work on the pumps."

"To get up an appetite for breakfast?"

"Sure. We keep bailing until the meal is cooked and the grub eaten. Then we swim out to the barn and twist a cow's tail so that she turns over to be milked. When we finish we give a reverse twist and right 'er. Our hens are learning to lay eggs in the eaves too. Next year we hope to teach the cows to swim up to the house to be milked."

Kercheval was beyond humor at the flood's vagaries. He did point out that from his ranch to the wing dam, a distance of eight miles, the levees were in perfect condition. The only break on the Old River side was where the water poured across Steamboat Slough and cut away the levees on the inside. "They *must* go higher," said Reuben Kercheval, and began another campaign when the waters receded.

But he found an apathetic, almost resigned Grand Island. His sons were older now and they fought with him for the levees. But the odds were against them. The rest of the islanders planted crops, took chances on the high water, and refused to fight the river. Kercheval took horses and scrapers and the inevitable Chinese and began doggedly to rebuild the levees. He did not live to see the clamshell dredgers drop their steel buckets into the river in 1889 and exult as their long steel arms groped landward and dumped sand upon the stout levees. But his sons and grandsons were there. The largest clamshell dredgers in the world came to the river, the *Hercules* and others like it. They moved as much in one day as five hundred Chinese and Kanakas and Indians had for Kercheval. And they did it for four cents a cubic yard.

In 1890 the river made a last effort to best the dredgers. Water went over the levees, but the machines built so swiftly and so well thereafter that even the great flood of 1907 was held at bay. Grand Island stands now as Reuben Kercheval dreamed it, a garden secure from the river, more fertile even than he imagined. A quarter century ago Howard Kercheval, Reuben's son, saw his men pack 11,000 boxes of luscious pears from the fruit trees of 22 island acres. In 1939 *his* son had a great yield.

Reuben Kercheval is gone. But his grandsons and his great-grandsons, his granddaughters and his great-granddaughters, still live on Grand Island and the river. They love the land and there will be Kerchevals on the river as long as there are Kerchevals. Great dredgers now deepen the channel each day and the land along the river is irrigated by the same waters against which Kercheval built his dikes. The river and its tributaries lend their strength to man the great pumping plants that water the rich soil. These same pumping plants, powered by the river, drain the land of surplus rains in the springtime. The Sacramento tames itself today.

10

Immediately after the discovery of gold men began to think about methods of mining. Worthless gadgets milled about the diggings, along with workable devices. One invention that promised easy fortune was the "goldboat," a dredge that would reach down into the river beds and shovel up golden gravel with mechanical thoroughness and in such quantities that even low-grade material would be worth mining. The first goldboats were failures. But the thought of the gold waiting in the rich river channels was too alluring to let men forget the scheme, regardless of the disappointments and hazards involved. Determined experimenters kept at it, continually improving the machines.

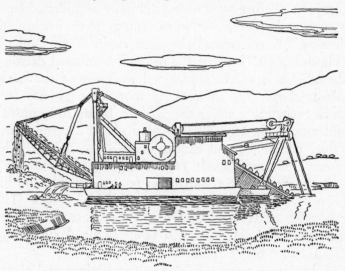

An Englishman in Australia, in 1875, perfected a bucket dredge that operated with the buckets on an endless chain. Two years later the Risdon Iron Works of San Francisco built and operated the same type of goldboat on the Yuba, the first dredge made in California. This Risdon dredge was mechanically perfect but, like a succession of similar ventures in the same region, it did not operate profitably because of the great depth of pay gravel. "Like sweepin' glue up with a broom," wailed "Pop" Harbison, one of the luckless operators. "You get every dam' thing figgered out that kin possibly happen—an' Lady Luck kicks you in the face with somethin' new!"

A fruitgrower named W. P. Hammon had a hunch about the puzzling business. For a few years before and after 1900 he and a half dozen friends experimented with dredges near Oroville, never breaking even but forever tinkering with new machinery and ideas. Hammon was bothered by worse things than inadequate dredges. Miners termed the great basin of the Yuba a "blind deposit" because the ore was blanketed deep by the tailings from the abandoned workings of the Little Giants above. The slickens lay more than twenty feet thick everywhere above the rich ore. It had to be moved and moved cheaply. Tests were made to determine the value, character, and extent of the gravel beds. The money Hammon made from his orchard went back into the ground faster than his fruit grew. He and his friends were gambling against hidden jokers. The profitable gravel was known to lie at least ninety feet below water level. That was twice as far down as any ground then being dredged.

Hammon spent $60,000 in test borings and a survey of the river-gravel belt. Then he built two more goldboats, adding several new practical features that he had designed. Those gulping dredgers were the first money-making machines to pull up the golden gravel from the upper Sacramento tributaries. After them came a swift succession of new dredgers and new owners, battling sometimes side by side for the treasure. The first dredger hulls were made of wood and cost $100,000. The later ones were built of steel at a cost of a half million dollars each. Towns sprang up at Hammonton and Marigold, where the dredger people lived. Guggenheim interests competed with the owners of the first machines and many small companies operated one dredger each. Today millions in gold are dredged annually from the Yuba and Feather river sections. A decade ago estimates put the probable life of paying gravel at ten years. Today the same estimate is quoted. The chances are that dredging will be profitable for another quarter of a century.

Occasionally the Yuba acts up and throws gold dredgers about as if they were tin toys. In December of 1937 a goldboat five miles below Oroville capsized when the river was in flood and a dozen others were driven from their moorings. Goldboat owners are often at swords' points with their neighbors. A thundering row developed in the next year on the Trinity River near Weaverville when the charge of mining pollution was thrown at the dredge operators. The battle was so bitter that the dredgers agreed to quit operating until equipment could be installed to protect the river from their tailings. The dredgers are once more active now, but the stream is protected from their silt.

In Trinity County, too, the only place where the Anti-Debris Act did not reach, the Little Giants still cut gold from the gravel banks. This is the last stand of the "earth shakers," but they are off the beaten path and few know, or care, that they still exist.

PART FOUR

The Imperishable Land

I

Long ago, while covered wagons still moved slowly west, a sea of wheat covered the Sacramento Valley. It rose out of the rich earth and the harvest meant bread for the world and cake for the men who reaped it. For forty years it spread ever more widely. There was no wheat country in the world like the Sacramento lands. Then, after 1850, it shrank to tiny, lakelike patches, dried up by the Kings of Wheat who were the most colossal spenders of resources in our history. For fifty years the land had been sown to the same crop and it was tired.

Sutter sowed the first wheat in the valley and set the first threshing machines to work, the hoofs of his wild mares. But he was gone from Hock Farm and pleading his case to Congress before the wheat era reached its zenith and twenty men owned a million acres among them. Joe Spencer Cone came from Marietta, Ohio, had a hard trip across the plains, swung a pick at Ophir, cut "shakes" from sugar pines for fifty dollars a day, and finally owned a hundred thousand acres of the river valley. Dr. Hugh James Glenn, a Virginian, crossed and recrossed the plains thirteen times before he raised a million bushels of wheat one year and chartered his own fleet of vessels to take the crop to Liverpool where he liked the prices better. John

Boggs, later California State senator, came from Potosi, Missouri. He was a man who didn't believe in compromise. Even when a new county line put the Boggs mansion in Colusa County and the barns in Glenn County the righteous Boggs was able to change the map in a twinkling and the livestock were put back in the same county with the Boggs parlor.

These, and a few others, were the captains of the wheat era. They wanted their own way and usually got it, making their own rules whenever possible. The swaying grain in the wide fields convinced them that big harvests would be endless. Year after year they planted wheat, never replenishing the earth with a different crop. Even when the end was inescapably near they were stubborn and slow to acknowledge that the soil was impoverished. They were against dividing their vast fields in a new and more abundant cycle of diversified farming.

Joe Cone was the shrewdest of those who ruled the wheat era. He was a bargainer, acquisitive and direct, as forceful as a keg of powder and a tireless worker. At twenty he left his farm home near Marietta to trade the Cherokees right out of their moccasins. When the news of gold came he joined an overland party and started west. On the way the Piutes stole the horses and the party found itself on foot and hungry. Cone reached Nevada in 1850 and tried his hand at some unsuccessful placer mining near Ophir. After that he freighted miners' supplies from Sacramento to Nevada. This was more to his liking; he could charge as much for a shovel as another man could pay. He went back to Ohio in November of 1853. California needed cattle and he knew where he could buy them cheap. The next year he returned with a trail herd the sale of which put $7,000 in his pockets. Cone then had the idea that raising wheat on a large scale might make him a millionaire quicker than mining or trading.

He bought land on Alder Creek, in Tehama County. The mining towns were paying top prices for beef and mutton and the good prospects carried him into the stock-raising business. Joe Cone began to grow rich, and meanwhile the wheat idea sprouted greener and higher in his mind. He had married Colonel Reppert's only daughter on one of his trips to Ohio and he wanted the security of a farm for his children. So he set his mind on wheat.

First, he needed more land. Luckily he caught the owners of Rancho Molinos cursing a tax demand of $50,000. "Why, the whole ranch isn't worth that much!" swore Woodworth, one of the pair.

"Would you take fifty thousand in cash for it?" asked Cone mildly, who was sure Woodworth was bluffing.

"I would."

"Here's your money," said Joe Cone. And wrote out a check.

In this fashion he became the master of a hundred thousands acres of some of the richest soil in the state. The borders of the property ran south along the east bank of the Sacramento River for fourteen miles from a point near Red Bluff, then east for a dozen miles across the valley into the foothills and back against the mountains. Antelope Creek and Mill Creek ran through the parklike land where huge oaks stood like sentinels. The underbrush was thick, and the land needed clearing, but that could be done in time. The wheat would

come. Joe Cone had what he wanted and he went to
work.

He built two rancho headquarters, six miles apart.
"Red Mike" Lafferty superintended the clearing of the
land. Orchards and gardens were set out to feed the
hired hands; later they sent most of their produce to
the nation. Fifty thousand sheep soon grazed on stubble
and lush grasses, their summer range the mountain
reaches of Lassen County.

This sheep business also was notably profitable for
Joe Cone. He almost doubled his investment in one
good year. Sheep had increased in numbers since the
middle of the century, but were decimated like the
great cattle herds by the drought of 1864 when more
than one-third of the cattle and sheep from San Diego
to Red Bluff died for lack of grazing and water. But
the sheep came back as wool and mutton prices rose,
and today sheep raising is an important industry. Although the drought was disastrous for the cattle herds,
it was not one season's lack of rain, but the rising cost
of land, the development of railroads, the growth of
population, and the fencing of the ranges that diverted
interest from stock raising.

Cone and the rest of the wheatgrowers found that
grain was the logical substitute for cattle. No irrigation
was necessary. Grain was not dependent on local markets; the world wanted it. The long, hot summers of the
valley produced a hard, dry wheat that could stand
months of transport to Europe without shrinkage or
spoilage. There was little chance of rain in the harvesting season and the sacked grain could be safely left in
the open fields until shipment.

At the times of sowing and harvesting Joe Cone's

fields, it was as if an army were in the fields. More than five hundred men were busy at harvesttime. A fifth of that number worked the year round in the gardens and orchards and fields. Hundreds of thousands of bushels of wheat were sacked each year. Hundreds of thousands of pounds of wool were sheared for market.

The increased use of machinery gave him greater scope. He set out ten thousand Bartlett pear trees although he was sure that wheat was the thing. No good wheatgrower allowed himself to see fruit raising as a profitable venture threatening the supremacy of grain. Joe Cone's fingers were dipped into a score of certainties. With Charles Cadwallader he established the Bank of Tehama County. With Major Kimball he brought into being the Cone, Kimball Company, largest mercantile house in the Red Bluff region. He loaned money to found the Antelope Flume and Lumber Company, first firm to transport logs by the V flume in California. The venture failed. Joe Cone gathered it in and promptly it became the Sierra Flume and Lumber Company, rafting lumber down the river from Red Bluff.

Lumbering had its short day on the Sacramento before good roads and rails took the logs to market quicker and cheaper than the curving streams. Not since the eighties have huge lumber rafts rolled down the river, shooting rapids and braving the perils of Three Rocks in Iron Canyon, above Red Bluff. That part of California's lumber saga is ended. Simon Darrah, Irvin Ball, Frank Farrow, and their fellows, those boisterous raft riders of early years, have finished their river business. Those who follow their calling are wheeling trucks along cement highways with sleepy eyes.

The rafts began their passage from many river points. The high-water shipping point belonged to the M. B. Vilas Lumber Company at Logan's Ferry above the mouth of Bear Creek, opposite Fort Reading. Ox teams hauled millions of feet of lumber to the river there. Raftsmen cut deep auger holes into key planks, tamped them with wooden pegs to hold the rafts together. Indians often watched the progress of the heavily laden rafts from the banks but no arrow ever impeded the wooden parade. Perhaps the red man was a trifle awed by the sight of his fallen forest on its voyage to help raise an alien empire on Indian land. At Marysville and Sacramento and San Francisco the cargo and rafts themselves were sold and along the river today one can find auger holes in stout old structures, proof that pegged lumber came swirling down the Sacramento, guided by song and pike pole and giants' arms.

Joe Cone liked the role of grand seigneur, the human feeling of power, whether it came from directing lumber or wheatgrowing or banking. No amount of "soft-dawder" changed his mind. When Joe Cone was right he was right, and that was the end of it. He was a Republican who hated Secession, Copperheads, interference, people who gave him advice, and people who didn't. His Presbyterian sense of proprieties grew with the years and he detested "mountebanks who want to run God and the country, either in Sacramento or Washington."

Finally, in the late seventies, in despair at the freight rates throttling California shippers, he subtly boosted himself into the position of president of the Railroad Commission. Proving that the Cone shrewdness still held, a number of historians now speak in milk-and-honey accents of Joseph Spencer Cone who was "drafted in the crisis, surprised and hesitant at the honor heaped upon his protesting head, yet heeding duty's call with all the magnificent determination at his command."

In 1880 Joe Cone reduced freight rates for California wheat, wool, and fruits by one-third. It was a good fight and he enjoyed it. To compete with foreign and eastern markets, California farmers had to have that reduction.

It is interesting to find that Joe Cone knew when his kingdom had grown too large for him. That must have been a sad day, even if the years had brought him some measure of tolerance and patience. Only a wise man decides to divide his kingdom before it is done for him. Joe Cone had the wisdom to begin his subdividing in 1890, while he still had time. He owned the great sweep of the Rio de los Molinos rancho and he was determined that the men who took the small patches of it must keep the land fruitful. In sympathy with change, he put a turbine on Antelope Creek and lighted his home, his barns, and incidentally the city of Red Bluff, with electricity.

Joe Cone is gone, but the memory of his crisp tempers, his shrewdness, and his hope still lives. He had a frontier flavor in him and his eagerness for the land was not petty.

Hugh Glenn, less single-minded than Cone, was a romantic youngster when the Mexican War whirled him against Chapultepec and sent him home a hero in Nancy Abernathy's eyes. He graduated at the head of his class from Cooper Medical College in 1849 and married Nancy. Then young Dr. Glenn decided, suddenly, that he didn't want to be a doctor. A man could grow gray in medicine and still be poor. He started overland to the country where gold was so plentiful that men grew rich in a day. He promised to return soon. The next year he brought back $5,000 and bright tales to a delighted young wife. Hopes high, he put the money into a Missouri bank the day before it failed.

Leaving Nancy and their young son in St. Louis, he turned west again. In 1851, his luck in mining still holding, he brought them to live on Putah Creek, in Yolo County. California was "home" now, Nancy wrote her mother. Hugh Glenn began to raise wheat and stock, trying and discarding partnership. Between ceaseless cattle trips to the East, he bought land on the northern end of the Jacinto rancho in what was to be Glenn County. There came a time when Hugh Glenn, who had forsaken the scalpel for the land, saw eighty thousand of his acres rolling in a golden haze, saw a million bushels of wheat harvested in one season on his ranch although that same year a north wind whipped a million dollars' worth of wheat into the ground.

Hugh Glenn was unpredictable, full of swift resentments and decisions. The 1880 wheat prices did not suit him. He chartered a dozen ships, took ten days to stuff their holds with his million bushels of grain, and then set sail for Liverpool. He made his own bargain there and come back with his cabin full of English gold, the only payment he would accept.

Glenn tired of his great Nevada cattle ranch and sold it to Miller and Lux for a quarter of a million dollars. He kept the French-Glenn Cattle Ranch in Oregon with its 150,000 acres. He ran for the governorship of California and grinned when George Perkins, the successful candidate, sent "our omnipotent Wheat-King back to the farm." He came to be a power in the State Board of Agriculture, but he died before the tide of wheat had reached its peak and never knew that the black soil he liked to crumble in the palm of his hands as he walked through stubble fields was being drained of fertility by his own insatiable demands for a single crop.

John Boggs, the senator, was the most assertive of this fraternity. Fresh from Fayette College he mined Weber Creek until he was starved into being a chainman on the first survey gang at work in Sacramento City. He put a few dollars into land on Cache Creek and began trading for broken-down horses and mules that incoming emigrants felt they had no further use for. They were eager for provisions and supplies and privately considered talkative young Mr. Boggs a dunderhead. Johnny wintered his stock that year and sold it for $200 a head in the spring. With that money he went into Colusa County and bought six thousand acres of the Larkin grant.

Wheat and stock raising and politics were Johnny Boggs's business and he succeeded in everything he tried. He financed banks, made enemies, became a state senator, and enjoyed life. He was a member of the Board of Trustees of Stanford University and a regent of the University of California. And he was one of the few first rulers of the golden sea who lived to see the impoverishment of the valley and grow strangely soft-voiced over the foolish fancies of his youth.

When the gold hunters first came there was no wheat for them. Oregon sent what could be spared. Australia did its bit. So did Chile—800,000 barrels of

SACRAMENTO
WHEAT BARGES

flour in the five years after '49. Prices rocketed up or down, depending on the supply at hand.

But the scene was reversed after '54. Wheat was being shipped out of the valley to Oregon and China and Mexico. Australia was having a gold rush of her own and calling anxiously for Sacramento's plump-kerneled grain. California was even sending wheat to Chile!

Scores of small flour mills sprang up in the valley. Wheat prices were fairly stable by the time Sumter was fired on. Shipments were even being made to England, the beginning of the mighty export trade of later years. Drought and flood and war in various of the earth's corners in the sixties caused curious fluctuations in wheat prices. The year that Lee turned his horse homeward from Appomattox it was a common thing for ships carrying cargoes of New York wheat to San Francisco to pass ships laden with California wheat bound for New York.

Throughout the seventies Liverpool, paying generous prices, took all of California's wheat. Englishmen named it "California White Velvet" and proclaimed it the best in the world. These were the fat and profitable days. More acres were hurriedly put into wheat. All of it was water-borne then, mostly by foreign ships. In 1889 the state led the nation in wheat production, more than fifty million bushels. And the Kings of Wheat knew that the prosperous years would never end!

Timesaving devices were important in the later days. Gang plows and steam tractors cut prices of production. Combination harvesters and threshers marched across the fields, cut the grain, threshed it, bagged it, and sewed it up in sacks. Sometimes the straw was fed to the engine as fuel. Where engines were not used, long lanes of horses, 22 to 32 of them, hitched together in a maze of harness, drew the threshers.

Steam and expensive machinery pushed the little fellows into the hands of the Kings of Wheat. Small farms were gobbled up and added to the imperial holdings of the few. No small owner could long compete against the economic royalists who forced large-scale production on the land. This concentration of wheat acreage went on until the Kings of Wheat were supreme: in 1892 less than a hundred men owned 1,600,-000 acres of Sacramento Valley land. But the end of the era was upon them, even then. In that same year the yield of the tiring soil was a third lower than the year before. By 1906 wheatgrowing was actually an unprofitable venture. Land values had increased, taxes were higher, the country more thickly settled. The great landowners were becoming "land poor." Still another blow was the low price of wheat in England. In the nineties Liverpool wanted her supply from India; Argentina and Canada also were competing for the English market. Oregon went after the Oriental markets, forcing down the prices there.

The Kings of Wheat were finished, whether they liked it or not. Some of them lived to be surprised by a compensatory phenomenon: in the end, when the golden sea was almost gone, out of its dried-up acres rose a greater abundance than the first, the empire of vine and fruit and vegetable, diversified and fabulously abundant.

2

In late 1849 a bright young man came from Kentucky to California. He had three books on civil engineering and a knack for making himself useful. In no time at all he was piloting the first steam ferry to ply back and forth across Carquinez Strait, his books keeping him company in the wheelhouse. He was sixteen and the *Lucy Long* was a cranky vessel, given to hidden miseries and unexpected moments of leisure in midstream, with no respect at all for schedules. But he got along well enough with her. This ferry job was only one of his duties. One day a week he galloped over Sonoma and Napa counties, with the United States mail tucked in one flat pocket. There had been considerable talk in San Francisco when the second mail contract let in California was given to a beardless whippersnapper who always seemed to be nosing around for work when better men were resting. In the rush of affairs the objections were swiftly forgotten except, perhaps, where men sat on benches and had time to remember what irked them last week. The boy had no ear for small tempests, then or later. He went his way and he was always on the lookout, whether he stood in the *Lucy Long's* wheelhouse or moved about on shore. His forebears, mainly interested in the soil, had followed Daniel Boone's trail from Virginia west through the gateway of the Cumberland Gap into Kentucky. Will Semple Green had merely pushed farther west and his objective was still the land.

The boy from Kentucky wanted a number of things. He had as little formal education as an obscure young lawyer named Lincoln, from the same state, but be was chock-full of ideas. Will Green had no brief against gold; but he was certain that the land was the enduring thing. Gold was no seedtime harvest. Once reaped it was forever ended. The land would be the mother of green crops long after the gold was gone. And he felt it a silly business to stake everything for sudden fortune when the fields would bear as long as men had the wit, the vigor, and the urge to work them.

In July of 1850 he left the *Lucy Long* and his mail contract to someone with a beard. The new steamer *Colusa* needed a pilot for an upriver journey and he took the job. The river ran through rich land and that was where he wanted to go. The steamer paused to give her name to a townsite and young Will Green was enchanted by the glory of virgin fields he saw. The place suited him and the *Colusa* went back downstream with a new pilot.

Will Green liked people. He had a friendly and interested ear for everyone, a deference for each man's opinion, and a casual, agreeable way of making his own words slow to stir antagonism. Nobody quarreled with his fervencies about land. It was only when he began to grow persistent that something be done about summer drought that he met opposition.

Walking on land of your own is a great incentive to thought. Will Green did a lot of thinking anyway. The possession of rich, level acres made him aware that ownership is only a beginning. His first few years near the frontier village of Colusa showed him that in order to have the land reach its maximum fertility there must be irrigation against the normal drought of summer and drainage for the bottom lands in times of flood. This was a challenge to Will Green's ingenuity and resource.

There had to be a leader, he knew. Most of his neighbors were so busy with personal equations that they had to be backed into a corner and the mirror of the future held close to their eyes before they could see beyond the present.

Will Green kept at it. He made himself into a competent civil engineer because he wanted to master the problems of the land. He worked and studied, drew plans and talked quietly to people.

Before he was thirty Will Green was powerful in the community. In 1864 he put on paper the drawings for a canal that would bring Sacramento River waters to irrigate the dry plains. With increasing excitement he drew plans on the map of Colusa and Yolo counties that represented a great shipping canal a hundred feet wide. He estimated the cost at $12,000,000. Bankers and friends scurried away like frightened quail whenever Will Green got around to the costs. His canal never went from the pen to the shovel stage. But he was not disheartened. He never called failure by its name; "a slight postponement" was the way he referred to it.

For another twenty years he tried to get irrigation projects under way. In 1883 he called Senator John Boggs, N. D. Rideout, and H. B. Julian to Willows for a talk about the possibilities of Stony Creek. Will Green told the three that there was almost enough water in Stony Creek to irrigate the entire Sacramento Valley. He spread out compact plans on the table before them so that they could see the abundant waters flowing to the dry summer fields under their very eyes. Before they left the meeting room they had formed a tentative corporation and the funds were pledged to give Stony Creek its niche in Paradise, as Will Green phrased it.

But there were farmers along the creek who owned riparian rights and would not co-operate. They wanted a tiger's share of everything Will Green had planned. They could have got it, too, if his had been the last word. He wanted the green fields, not profits. But when the farmers presented their demands to the new company, Johnny Boggs, Rideout, and Julian called it stalemate and went on about their business. Once more Will Green had met "a slight postponement."

Some unwise legislation tried to smooth out difficulties and make it simpler for valley Irrigation Districts to be organized and operated. They read like puzzles and blocked the very action they were designed to aid. Most landowners were determined to muddle along in their own way. The Kings of Wheat laughed at Will Green's plans and went on systematically with their one-crop planting. Many farmers put in pumping plants of their own and watered those fields which could be easily flooded. The barge *Merritt* worked up and down the Sacramento, pumping water for the farmers who needed it. In a day's pumping the *Merritt* could cover eighty-eight acres a foot deep but she could deliver water only to lands near the river.

Will Green went ahead with his talk and his plans. Possessed of the logic and dry wit of a Ben Franklin, he was the first Californian to value land over gold. As an engineer he surveyed the land. As a legislator he drew up the land code of the state. As surveyor general of the United States he protected the public domain as a trust for the settlers who could till it. As treasurer of California he conserved the taxes paid by the owners of the land as if they had been funds out of his own pocket. In the pages of his *Colusa Sun* he wrote of the soil as the chief concern of men. "The imperishable land," he said, "has fed and clothed and housed us long before we held gold in our hands."

At the turn of the century Will Green had not accomplished what he hoped. Only a few of his fields were watered by the river. He had made his *Colusa Sun* the leading voice of the land in California. In the same connection he fought for the small farmer, claiming that a few men owned too much of the valley. "Small farms make homes and happiness and hope," he wrote. "God give us little farms in California."

When Will Green died in 1905, Irrigation Districts and canals and great pumping stations were still in the future. But he was sure they would come. "Not because it is an old man's dream," he wrote, "but because the land will pay men well for the water they bring to it."

The year before Will Green died a drayman named Burt from Crescent City hoisted his wife and six children into his cart, took his $1,000 in savings out of the bank, and turned his horses' heads in the direction of Princeton, in Colusa County. Once there, Burt made a payment on seven and a half acres of bottom land beside the Sacramento and went to work. He built his house and barn with his own hands. That first season he put three acres into alfalfa. Around the house he set out a small orchard. Between the trees he planted a vast variety of berries and vegetables. Under each tree he placed a beehive, hoping the bees would pollenize his orchard in the process of making honey. Every foot of his few acres was finally cultivated, watered by ditches he had dug. At one corner of his microscopic farm he had planted melons and corn, leaving barely enough room for a chicken yard, cowpen, and pigsty.

If Burt's neighbors paid any attention to him at all, it was to remark that he was cracked. To Princeton people a farm was upward of twenty thousand acres and seven and a half represented only a "garden patch." Intensive farming wasn't even a name to them. They would have "hooted down the river" any suggestion that Burt was beginning a new age for the Sacramento Valley. But six years later Burt of Princeton had made the final payment on his home. He had never borrowed a dollar and he was banking a tidy sum each year. On his farm he had 240 peach trees, 110 pear trees, 5 apricot and 5 cherry trees, 2 crabapple and 8 fig trees, 7 nectarine and 14 orange trees, 8 lemon and 5 walnut trees, 200 grapevines, 100 loganberry vines, and 300 mammoth blackberry vines. He had two brood sows and their 23 fat progeny, 7 cows, 5 sheep, 3 horses, and 100 chickens. That sixth year Burt paid all his bills and put more than $2,000 in the bank. Woodland Wilhelmina, a registered Holstein, was chewing her cud contentedly in the barn with his small herd. She was the Grand Prize awarded by the Sacramento Valley Irrigation Company to the man with the best-developed farm in its service borders.

Will Green, the "Father of Irrigation," would have been delighted by Burt's farm. But there was a joker hidden in Burt's success. The Kuhn Banking Syndicate of Pittsburgh took one look at his land and poured ten million dollars into a quarter of a million acres in Glenn and Colusa counties, under a comprehensive irrigation system. It was only the beginning. The Kings of Wheat and their extensive dry-land kingdom gave way to great intensive farms that were equally large. Burt had shown the way to a new kind of farming in which men and science renewed the soil in a productive partnership. Will Green's small farms were to exist. But along with them were to be the food factories with a huge output, the holdings of the few.

The story of fruit has been the story of lands made fertile by irrigation, of orchards and vineyards appearing where there had been grainfields, cattle ranges, and even desert stretches. Today millions of grapevines grow on the valley floor. From them come wine grapes, table grapes, raisin grapes, and other varieties. Hundreds of thousands of orchard acres, peach, apricot, pear, apple, prune, nectarine, plum, cherry, fig, olive, walnut, almond, orange, and lemon trees flourish. Canning and dried-fruit industries have grown up around them. Refrigerator cars, airplanes, and ships carry the produce to world markets. Asparagus, beans, melons, sugar beets, berries, tomatoes, alfalfa, rice, and all types of vegetables are great crops along the river and in the valley. And each of these, from grape to asparagus, has an important story of its own.

Men brought all this into being. They found as much romance and hardship along the pioneer trail of intensive farming as the mountaineers had discovered fighting their way west. They were, and still are, battling insect pests and vagaries of climate, studying the chemistry of the soil, using fertilizer, and spraying chemicals on parasitic life forms. When the cottony-cushion scale came from Australia to endanger the California citrus groves, the scientists ferreted out *Novius cardinalis,* a not too-respectable ladybird beetle, to destroy the destroyer. The scientists have invented smudgers and heaters to circumvent frost. They have learned ways to fertilize the Kadota fig and give new impor-

tance to one of the state's oldest fruits. When the
Japanese beetle made its entry into America, another
imported parasite was introduced to kill the beetle. The
scientists have "air-conditioned" the citrus groves,
devised air chambers to fight San José scale, and they
have seeded land by airplane. They have always been
on their toes to meet hazards and they are constantly
writing a new chapter of success as they keep the vines
and trees and vegetable beds in a balanced seasonal
abundance.

3

The oldest Chinese temple in America stands near
the Sacramento River, in Marysville. In the temple live
Kwang Kung, goddess of mercy, Choi Sun, goddess of
finance, and the potbellied, ever-smiling god of fortune,
Gai Foo. They have been there since their worshipers
carried them across a sea and over a great valley to the
"Great Gold Mountain," to their new shrine. They have
seen strange events yet remained aloof in gilt and lac-
quered calm. They look upon a century as a passing
dream in the spring. Indeed, is it not written that man
is as short-lived as frost upon a tiled roof? They are
heavenly philosophers, Kwang Kung, Choi Sun, and Gai
Foo, and they need to be. For those who worshiped
them have walked through dark and dangerous days
since golden treasure called them to California.

The first Chinese legions found an almost royal
welcome in San Francisco. When the city celebrated
California's admission as a state, one of the most color-
ful parts of the long parade was a group of richly
dressed Chinese in native costume, bearing a huge blue
silk banner inscribed: "The China Boys." The state

needed workmen and these newcomers were a ready answer to the problem. Associations known as the Six Companies brought most of the Chinese to California. The laborers were transported under a system of contract: their passage was paid and they agreed to work for a stated term at fixed wages, their freedom being guaranteed when each man had paid all claims against him. The associations had their own tribunals and dispensed justice as they saw fit regardless of the laws of California. Their "hatchet men" murdered any offender against the codes of the brotherhoods.

Swiftly the Chinese left their ships for laundries, shops, restaurants, the building trades, and the mines. The leaders of the Six Companies were being feted in San Francisco while the first "Foreign Miner's Taxes" were being garroted from Chinese miners in the foothills. Chinese laborers cooked in the camps, worked their own claims, washed out tailings abandoned by dissatisfied white miners who had moved on, helped build levees for Kercheval and his kind, and labored in the fields, orchards, and vineyards. Their leaders even became independent contractors for mining ditches and flumes where cheap labor was indispensable. The Chinese came from their native land like an engulfing torrent and soon they were hated and despised by the men who had welcomed them so gladly.

But the worshipers of Gai Foo were patient men, and persistent. They survived persecution and Exclusion Acts and discriminatory business practices. They built a Chinese quarter in San Francisco where jade and tapestries and lesser knickknacks could be sold, where a Chinese could feel at home among the odors and the customs, the tongues and the gods of his native land.

Many grew rich and powerful. Some of them became house servants in white families, beloved, dictatorial, and loyal. Their children went to American schools as well as Chinese. And the years, which are of slight account to Gai Foo, ran by swiftly.

In the beginning, when gold was the only business in California, they held doggedly to their dress and customs in an unfriendly and unpredictable land. The Chinese miners wore huge, wide-brimmed, conical-topped reed hats. Their shirts were double-breasted with the buttons down the sides and their trousers were loose and flowing. In time they put on American-made overalls for heavy work in the creek bottoms but they kept their shirts and hats. These shirts were elegantly long, extending almost to their knees, but they disposed of that length by tucking the tails inside their trousers, which were held up by a sash that served also as a money belt. Their queues caused more curiosity, speculation, and deviltry in their white neighbors than any other imported peculiarity. The Chinese who kept his queue when playful white miners with a few sharp knives were around was lucky indeed.

The Chinese miners in the foothills could not carry as many powerful gods with them as there were in the temple at Marysville. But each group had a bronze Buddha, secure in a small shrine, to which were made offerings of sweetmeats, rice brandy, and roast pig. It is a very comforting thing for a man to have at least one of his gods close to him in a strange land, a god who will understand and, perhaps, protect him when strangers may not.

The yellow miner was robbed and beaten by unscrupulous white men, and sometimes murdered for his slight store of treasure. Officials often treated the Chinese as harshly as the lawless miners, raiding their camps, ripping open rice sacks, wrecking their simple dwellings. If not enough gold was found to pay the exorbitant Foreign Miner's Tax, the hapless yellow men were tied to trees by their pigtails and beaten viciously. Chinese life and property were cheap during the gold days. And the gods who saw such atrocities without losing their ancient calm must also have been long-suffering.

During the period of hydraulic mining more heed was paid to Chinese rights. There was less of the old frontier brutality. White men had begun to respect the Chinese as good citizens and honest, diligent workmen who appreciated kindness and fair treatment. As tolerance increased, personal friendships began to grow up. No Chinese festival day passed at which children of friendly white families did not eat candies and sweetmeats brought from China, as well as vegetables and pickled pork from the festive tables. At the same time, the Chinese recognized Christmas as a day of cheer and universal goodwill, of giving and receiving, and they began to understand some of the virtues of these no longer strange people with whom they had chosen to live. For if men are to become part of a nation's life they must be close to its heart and mind and speech. The Chinese who came to America during the nineteenth century are now proud of being Americans.

Later than the Chinese came the industrious sons of Dai Nippon. Of all the Oriental emigrants, the Californians soon hated them the most. The Japanese had lived in splendid isolation until America's Commander Matthew Calbraith Perry sailed into their principal port in 1853 with a few gunboats, bent on beginning friendly relations. It took the Japanese some time to make up their minds to visit the nation across the sea of which Commander Perry spoke so glowingly. But when they did come they arrived in great numbers looking for land. They spread out into the Great Valley and around the cities. Working with the soil, they grew garden produce for half what it cost a white man.

The same weapons were used against them that had been used earlier against the Chinese, and laws were passed regulating their ownership of land. Chinese and Japanese simply lived more cheaply and were content with a lower wage than a white man. With Hindus, Filipinos, and Mexicans, they were the first laborers to serve in great numbers the growing empire of fruit and vine.

The Chinese and Japanese did not come to us empty-handed. They brought the wisdom of poets and philosophers, culture garnered from many centuries, their own forms of the theater and pictorial art, and an intense faith in the enduring value of craftsmanship and artistry. From them have come important gifts to the civilization and development, the drama and folklore of the river. Born of the land now and committed to its ideals and way of life, they are no longer alien. In the beginning their fathers came from Asia, as yours and mine came from Europe. But now they are Americans.

4

For a half century laborers in the Great Valley have followed the crops as they came into season. Today nearly a quarter of a million migrants work up and down the valley as one crop matures after another.

These migrants are an economic necessity to California's harvests. When the passing of one day can mean the loss of an entire perishable crop, the workers of this mobile army represent the difference between plenty and absolute crop failure. They are as necessary to the land as water and sun and seed. Without them the land is nothing.

For years these workers were Chinese, Japanese, Hindus, Mexicans, and Filipinos. They were mainly fruit pickers. About the time cotton became important as an industry to the southern part of the valley, fruit pickers grew less in numbers. The Mexicans were officially discouraged or became interested in their own government's planned economy for Mexican land. The Japanese and Chinese were farming for themselves. Only the Filipinos, living a hundred and twenty strong under canvas cubicles seventy feet square, still served the growers. Fortunately for the men who grew California's cotton, an additional supply of field labor found its way into the state from the cottonlands of the Southwest, to join the seasonal parade up and down the valley. These were the laborers on the river lands when nature made a Dust Bowl in the heart of America and forced a migration that is as old to earth as the tread of human feet.

Literally blasted out of their acres by dust and drought, thousands from the stricken regions turned their eyes to California. They gathered together all that the Gods of Devastation had left them and set out to begin again with an incurably American optimism. They came in ancient automobiles and asthmatic trucks, some of them homemade, an occasional rickety trailer careening behind. All their belongings were piled in and on the cars and covered with tattered bedding and worn canvas. With bedsprings on top, a heat-humped cookstove riding the running board, with the trunk and iron washtub tied on behind, the families consisting of children, wives, aunts, grandmothers, grandfathers, fathers, stray cousins, were wadded closely into the available

space inside. These newcomers to the valley, unlike the first tide of single workers, were men with families.

Nine of ten in this army were white Americans. They were victims of nature's cataclysmic humors, dust storms and drought, and of man-made depressions that preceded the drought. Their journey had been bitter. They did not represent a collection of failures, beaten by laziness, dishonesty, and shiftlessness. They were, quite simply, human beings cruelly dislocated by the process of social erosion. Like their once rich soil, they had been scattered by mighty winds. Some had been "tractored out" by the machine, tenant farmers from Texas. But they had faith in the soil and their dreams were kept alive by the belief that, someday, they were sure to walk and work again on land they could call their own. So the files of top-heavy vehicles kept on coming to California. White Americans supplanted the Chinese, Japanese, Hindus, Mexicans, and Filipinos who had once farmed California's intensive crops.

In the last half of 1935, 43,000 rolled into California on thin tires. A year later 100,000 came and in 1937 an equal number. The influx slackened after that. Most of them were refugees from Texas, Oklahoma, Arkansas, and Arizona. A few returned to the states of their origin, but not many. They had come to the last physical frontier of the country—beyond California lies the Pacific.

In the wheat days intensive farming produced only four per cent of California's agricultural output. Now it represents more than eighty per cent and an annual half billion dollars. From the valley comes nearly half the world's fresh fruit, nearly all its dried fruit, and three-fourths of its canned fruit and vegetables. This, then, is the real urgency behind the demand for mobile labor in the Great Valley.

With the intensive cultivation of the fruit trees, vineyards, and vegetables have come highly capitalized, large-scale farming methods and concentrated ownership. The entire valley presents industrialized agriculture; a system of open-air food factories. Sixty per cent of America's biggest truck, poultry, and fruit farms are found in California alone. This type of farming passes on welcome economies to the American public's pocketbook in food prices and, at the same time, dispenses labor headaches. California, with the most highly mechanized farming system in the world, produces a paradox. Two-thirds of the state's farms are less than fifty acres. These are Will Green's "small farms," busy and profitable as he hoped they would be.

Men will never make machines that will pick apricots, peaches, or pears from heavy, wood-propped branches, or tomatoes, peas, and berries in the watered fields. Men's hands must serve the valley as long as there are crops and the personal problems of living for the caravan of the careworn will have to be met.

5

Near Kennett, a few miles above Redding, thousands of men and machines are blocking the Sacramento River with a dam twice as long as Boulder Dam and higher than Grand Coulee. This great barrier is the key unit of the Central Valley Project, Uncle Sam's $170,-000,000 conservation enterprise. It is designed to regulate and store the once lost floodwaters of the Sacramento and San Joaquin, which now will assure fertility to a two billion dollar agricultural empire stretching from Shasta to the Tehachapi and from the Sierras to the sea. The dam has been named Shasta in honor of the peak that towers whitely near the Sacramento's source. Here the river waters will back up for thirty-five miles into a huge lake, where they will be ready for use each year in the rainless summer.

Held behind the dam which rises 560 feet above the river bed, these reserve waters will give a year-round stability to a river that runs with a dozen times the intensity of the Mississippi. The dam will leash forever the fury of springtime floods and prevent the sluggish currents and low water of late summer. Boats will find the river always navigable to Red Bluff and there will be a constant flushing of the salt-troubled Delta region. A limitless supply of fresh water will race through the Delta Cross Channel to the Contra Costa Canal and the San Joaquin pumping system. Hydroelectric energy generated at Shasta Dam will flash down two hundred miles to Antioch and there it will operate the pumps that lift fresh water to the valley land.

The San Joaquin, carrying only one-fourth the volume of the Sacramento, cannot irrigate much of the arid area through which it flows. Water from the Sacramento must be diverted through the San Joaquin pumping system, near Tracy, up the lower San Joaquin Valley as far as Mendota to supplement San Joaquin water released sparingly from Friant Dam, near Fresno. From Friant Dam the water will run north through the Madera Canal to the dry lands of Madera County, and flow south by way of the Friant-Kern Canal to parts of Fresno, Tulare, and Kern counties, once threatened with reversion to desert.

But Shasta Dam will do more than bring water to lands without it. In summer, when the stream is low, salt water works into the channels which irrigate 400,-000 highly developed acres of the rich Sacramento-San Joaquin Delta region. A pressure of fresh water, a year-round regulated flow from the lake behind Shasta Dam, will keep the salt out.

The construction of Shasta Dam will destroy Kennett, the old smelter town. When cities die, their graves, like those of men, are marked in different ways. Angkor Wat is its own monument in the Cambodian jungle. Desert sands are sometimes dug away to show the remains of cities that were great five thousand years ago. A penciled scrawl on a board set a foot high on a mount of rubbish in France, in 1918, read: "This was Etrepilly." But Kennett's epitaph will be "writ in water," for it will lie deep in the great lake behind the dam.

Kennett, perched in a steep canyon of the upper Sacramento Valley deep in the Klamath Mountains, began life as an emergency brake-testing station for trains. In the early 1900's an important gold and copper discovery brought sudden affluence to the microscopic town. The United States Mining and Smelting Company moved into Kennett and paid $750,000 for its claim. The village became a roaring boomtown, wide open and as full of life and color as a Roman candle lighted at both ends. Within a year four thousand men were working in Mammoth Mine by day and spending their money freely by night.

This was the beginning of Kennett's golden era. An assassin fired two bullets in the cobblestoned streets of Sarajevo and thereby engineered a new vitality for Kennett. The World War lifted copper prices over the highest recorded peaks. Mammoth Mine doubled its output and raised wages. All copper mined was actually clear profit; the mine was so rich in gold that the gold output more than paid operating costs.

The Armistice was the end of Kennett's glory. Copper prices fell at once and stayed down. For a time the town would not believe that its heyday was over. The miners had harsh words for local calamity howlers and started fist fights to prove that Kennett and its future were both strong and healthy.

But the miners did not have the final word. They offered to return to reduced pay and "normal conditions." The company turned the proposition down. Finally the owners were forced to close the Mammoth. The town was through and didn't know it. The miners laughed and predicted that "everything will open up soon."

The laughter cracked into silence when the Mammoth Mine disposed of all its working equipment and moved its corporate body to more profitable fields. A junking company dismantled the plant that had produced more than a hundred million dollars in ore.

In every boomtown and mining camp there are always a few die-hards who will not move on. Kennett had more than her share of them. There is a well-founded rumor in the region that they will put on diving suits and stay on when five hundred feet of water sloshes over the shingles. A score of these old-timers stayed on after the junking company carved up the Mammoth's bones. Even now, with twenty-five hundred men busy on Shasta Dam before their eyes, these stubborn believers in the good old days are still sure Kennett will "open up."

As night falls on Kennett, her old-timers should take some consolation in knowing that their town underwater will bring far more permanent good to California than she did when she was mining millions in ore. Sunset for Kennett means dawn for a million arid acres and new hope for countless human hearts. It should be enough for Kennett's stubborn champions.

However, they do not stand alone in their deprecation of Shasta Dam's promise. Recently a friend said to me, with a little laughter in his voice: "What if your river does make a million acres more fruitful? We'll soon be raising all our vegetables in a food factory with chemicals and a few tanks of water!"

Perhaps he is right. In this century even the land does not need as many of us as it did. But to produce a well-rounded human being takes just as much exposure to nature as ever. We need the land.

PART FIVE

River Days

I

CAPTAIN WILLIAM GAYNOR CORLETT came to the river in 1849. He had pile drivers for fists and he moved his big body over a deck with the grace of a tiger. He had bold eyes, a shrewdly river-wise brain, and was proud of having never struck a passenger without provocation. For thirty years he navigated the river and stories rolled plentifully in his wake.

Bill was the man who found two Chinese cook's helpers rifling a passenger's cabin aboard the *Defiance*. He tied their queues together with sailorlike dispatch, sloshed them overboard to the vast delight of a large audience, and then hoisted them up to the Texas deck and hung them out on a line to dry. He was seen ejecting "two ladies of frail repute" from the cabins of the *Chin-du-Wan* while the ship was still tied up to a Sacramento wharf. Picking one woman up under each arm, he walked to the river rail and dropped both bundles of flounces overboard, leaving them to reach the dock as best they could. He was the man who leaped into the river during a flood to save a yowling white cat and one kitten marooned on a pile of brush near the Washington City shore line. And he was "substitute" master of the *Goodman Castle* the day that he tied a half dozen iron plows together, hoisted them overboard at the end of a hawser, and drove his steamer up and down the Sacramento City water front in triumph, the first man to do undersea plowing to deepen a river bed. It worked, too. The swift stream promptly carried away the sand stirred up by Bill's plows.

These stories are true. But I am not sure about the tale of Bill's rescue of George Whipple's pure-bred bull off Sherman Island during the floods of '62. He

swam, according to eyewitnesses, from shore to boat safely swishing the bull by the tail behind him. He lifted the animal aboard with a cargo crane and gave it deck passage to Sacramento. Nor do I believe that he actually tossed Mr. John Phillip Courtney, the river gambler, from Mike Brady's saloon in Sacramento straight into a Chinese pump stream, forty feet away. Not that these feats were beyond Bill, but the record runs that he was at opposite ends of the river when they were supposed to have taken place.

Of course, Bill was a "mite peculiar," to quote

one of his contemporaries. Most of the river captains were soft-spoken passenger pleasers, long on patience and short on sharp words. So was Bill up to a certain point. But he had his own ideas about a captain's rights on his own deck and he drove more owners to open despair than any other master on the river. He was forever changing ships, by request. But he was one of the best skippers on the Sacramento and he always managed to find another berth. Bill never side-stepped trouble. He got into most of his difficulties because he believed, with vast assurance, that he could spot a thimblerig rascal by the cut of his jib, any day on any deck. Occasionally he was wrong. Usually that was the day he started looking for another ship.

Many rivermen and their craft had sailed the river before the steamer *McKim* carried Bill Corlett to Sacramento for the first time in September, 1849. John Sutter's *Sacramento* had been the most important river carrier until the 37-foot *Sitka* steamed to New Helvetia in 1847 before discarding its engine and becoming the sail-powered *Rainbow*. Sam Brannan had picked up a Chilian brig cheap, the *Eliodora*, and she was busy moving his goods to Sutter's Embarcadero. Hensley, Reading and Company owned the Peruvian bark, *Joven Guipuzcoana*. But these were small fry compared with Captain Gelston's *Whiton* of 241 tons, drawing eight feet of water, which sailed to Sutter's Embarcadero in May of '49, her royal yards crossed, and Pilot George Winner calling the channel. She was deep laden with merchandise consigned to R. Gelston and Company, from New York. The steamer *Sacramento*, stored in the hold of a brig, "in pieces," arrived in San Francisco harbor in July. Her owners rushed her together before a crowd of curious onlookers and Captain John Van Pelt skippered her upstream, the first American captain to bring a steamboat to the Sacramento River. Immediately behind him, much to his disgust, waddled another *Sacramento*, a reconverted scow with an engine in her.

The people of Sacramento turned out in holiday excitement when Captain Brenham edged the *McKim* into her wharf and Third Officer Bill Corlett got in more bellowed orders than the master. The shore ovation was for the "first *big* steamboat" to arrive there. Competition was hard in the *McKim's* wake, however. The steamer *Mint* came in October and ran between Sacramento City and San Francisco, touching at Benicia. There were thirty schooners, brigs, and barks in port when the *Mint* arrived. Then, in November, the "favorite daylight steamer *Senator*" made her initial trip under Captain Van Pelt, who had forsaken the smaller *Sacramento*. The steamer *Miner* rushed upstream in December, blowing her whistle ceaselessly as she went.

A few of the "Pony Powers," light-draught steamers, were making regular trips on the Yuba, Feather, and Upper Sacramento in 1849. The *New England, Aetna, Firefly,* and *George Washington* raced each other back and forth from upriver points to Sacramento, heavy with profitable trade hauls. The *George Washington* struck a snag above Vernon on one return trip and gave herself the doubtful honor of being the first Upper Sacramento casualty. She was raised in a few days and began her regular run, but was always "snag shy" thereafter, according to Captain Ben Galway.

The year Bill Corlett came to the river ended with nearly fifty boats plying the inland waterways. Some had names from distant parts of the world like the

Kanai and the *Sagadahock*. Other names were more personal, *Olivia, Diana,* and *My Darling.* And some had a lilt to them, *Sea Witch* and *Flame o' Dawn.*

There hardly was sea room between bows and sterns on the river in 1850. Not all the boats came from distant ports. California shipyards were born overnight and shipwrights worked every hour in the twenty-four. Speed was the driving word. The 120-foot steamer *Tehama,* with 40-horsepower double engines, was launched near Rincon Point on May 10, 1850, twenty days after her plans were drawn. Next day, when Captain Farwell and the *Tehama* reached Sacramento City the quays on both sides of the river were so crowded there was no place to dock. The sailing vessels lay two and three deep in places along the banks. Some were permanent storeships: Sam Brannan's *Joven Guipuzcoana* and the *Eliza* and the *Eliodora.* The *LaGrange* was a barnacled prison hulk. The number of sailing ships was many times that of 1849—barks, brigs, brigantines, and schooners. Among the new names were the *Quoddy Belle* of New Orleans, the *Arcadian* from Boston, the *Chesapeake* from Old Town, the *Sea Eagle* from Bombay, and the *Bag o' Bones* from London.

New steamers kept coming to the winding river in great numbers: the *Gold Hunter, El Dorado, Hartford, Governor Dana, Linda, Jack Hayes* and a score more. When the 1850 miner-carrying season was well under way a cutthroat competition began between the boats for the passenger trade. The most extraordinary promises and predictions were made for every "elegant and favorite steamer." Each boat had agents on the wharves or levee prior to the hour of departure, usually ship's officers or shore-living owners, who waged a warfare of words, and often of fists, over the merits of their respective packets. While Bill Corlett and Andy James were assuring the throngs of the *McKim's* speed, comfort, and safety, the most persuasive of the *Senator's* officers and backers a few feet away would be describing the *McKim* as nothing but a "dog-power propeller," a "junk," a "scow" with the rottenest bottom on the river. They would not forget to praise the "unsurpassed accommodations, unequaled celerity, and undoubted safety" of the *Senator,* or to boast of an eight-hour passage when they knew the boat would take twelve. Fares went down, of course, under this flood of passenger seeking. Rates fell from $30 to $10 and even lower.

In February, 1850, the *Senator* and *McKim,* each racing stubbornly to make the wharf first, collided with a mighty bang near Benicia. No damage was done except to stray bits of superstructure and sensitive nerves. Bill Corlett, second officer now since Captain Macy had taken over, leaped from the *McKim* to the *Senator* and disposed of the officers in her wheelhouse. He allowed himself to be pacified only after the *McKim* had edged into the landing ahead of her rival.

That spring Bill put $500 into a stock company that purchased the steamer *Phoenix* and fitted her up as the first gold dredger on the river. She was sent up the Yuba, beyond Marysville to Ousley's Bar, and began work. But her dredging machinery was faulty and the venture was a total loss for everyone concerned.

Bill had it in for gold dredging thereafter. Luckily for the original promoters of the scheme, none of them ever traveled on a Corlett boat following the *Phoenix* failure.

In the first month of 1851 steamboat fares between Sacramento and San Francisco fell to a dollar. Freight rates hit kindred lows. Every passenger craft raced up and down the river, boilers at bursting point, trying to lower the time schedule. Comfort also was a selling point. New steamers arrived from the East and no one living within blocks of a California shipyard got any sleep for the clatter of building. The steamer *Comanche* rolled off the ways from the Yolo side near Sacramento City just as the *San Joaquin* and *St. Lawrence* first nosed up the river. *The New World, Wilson G. Hunt, Antelope, Confidence, J. Bragdon,* and *Urilda* hurled themselves into the steamer parade. Captain Ike Warren brought the *Free Trade* into the competition with the good-will slogan: "We carry your children without charge." He even encouraged "picnic excursions under the most chaste and orderly dispensations." He had few well-wishers among the river skippers: Hutchins of the *New World*, Averill of the *Senator*, and *Poole* of the *Wilson G. Hunt* called him the "Children's Noble Friend" and once sent him a Christmas hamper filled with rosebuds and teething rings. Bill Corlett, lately first officer of the *Confidence*, also had nothing but a contemptuous word for Captain Warren. "Every day," said Bill, "he gets to look more and more like an old goat full of picnic sandwiches."

Big Business appeared on the scene early in 1854. The California Steam Navigation Company, organized by General A. A. Redington, Major Hensley, and a half dozen prominent boat captains, set out to control every type of river traffic. They began with the *Confidence, Colusa, Helen Hensley, New World, Sam Soule, Antelope,* and *Governor Dana*. In a few months they were making the going very rough for independent boats. From then on there was a continual effort by opposition steamers to outmaneuver the "gargantuan monopoly so horridly rampant in our midst."

No ingenious method of fighting went untried by either side. The opposition boats usually lacked capital to compete for long but they made life interesting for the company during their brief attempts. In 1855 the first appearance of the *Defender* as an opposition craft gave Sacramentans cause for excitement. There was no place for her to land on the ship-lined levee and she was finally moored temporarily to the store hulk, *Dimon*. Her lines were scarcely fast before the steamer *Pike*, due downriver and also moored to the *Dimon*, cast off and swung out into the stream. The *Defender* was at once moved in closer to take up the *Pike's* landing space. When her crew made fast they discovered that the *Pike's* departing gesture to the opposition cause had been to board up all gangway accommodations on the storeship. Deck hands had to take up axes and crash a way through stout oak timbers to unload passengers and freight.

Later, when her afternoon departure time drew near, the *Defender's* band started playing and "passengers were enticed aboard at a brisk pace." The band had played only a few minutes when a small stern-wheeler moved upstream and paddled close in to the *Defender*. When the band played, the stern-wheeler unloosed a sharp, shrill whistle blast that drowned out the music. When the band stopped, so did the whistle. When the band started again, so did the whistle. The band broke up temporarily and started hunting for shotguns. The crowd on the levee shouted angrily at the stern-wheeler.

On the levee three men and a half dozen boys were swinging raucous Chinese gongs, crying above both whistle and music the excellence of company boats. The din was so terrific that Judge Morrison, holding court near by, was forced to adjourn until the *Defender,* with her "enticed" passengers, moved out downstream for San Francisco.

For years the same show went on with variations. Sometimes spouting agents were pushed over the levee and on one occasion, the tiger having changed its stripes, Bill Corlett of the opposition threw three Chinese gongs into the river. There is no record as to whether the gong beaters went in with the gongs.

Light-draught steamers were carrying trade on the Yuba and Feather and Upper Sacramento and many "Merchants' Committees" built and fitted out opposition boats to handle their own supplies and produce. The *Enterprise* and *Queen City* were two such craft from Marysville and occasionally, in the heat of competition, fares fell to twenty-five cents between there and Sacramento. Captain Dave Hall, "broad of beam and mulish-minded," skippered the steamer *Linda* in the Upper Sacramento trade and the *Butte, William Robinson,* and *P. B. Reading* were competitors on the same stretch of river. It was the fashion to see which boat could run farthest upriver without disaster. The *Latona, Eureka, James Blair,* and *Maria* were built especially for this purpose; they drew only twelve to fourteen inches of water and they "skimmed the bars with contemptuous impunity." Captain Bart Keller of the *Maria* wrote this to his wife in Chicago a month before a snag took the bottom out of his skimmer below Red Bluff. The

Martin White joined the competition, towing behind her the first barge ever brought up the river.

A long succession of determined opposition boats fought a losing fight. For a few weeks in 1857 the *Ann McKim* and *Young America* forced fares to ten cents. The *Peytona* and *Goodman Castle* tried later, as did the *Princess* and *Cornelia* and then the *Victor* and *Milton S. Latham*. The bottom would drop out of rates for a few days; then with the ending of opposition schedules they would bounce up to irritating highs.

In the late months of 1859 and into the next spring a bar began to form in the Sacramento across the mouth of the American. It extended down to the Yolo bridge and became an increasing hazard and obstruction to river traffic. Everywhere in the upper tributaries of the Sacramento the channels, fed by the debris of the monitors higher up, had been steadily rising, building up bars here and there. Rivermen were as bitter as the stricken farmers who were appalled by the destruction upon them. The protest was deep and vengeful from the river and the farm lands but the miners let the roar of the Little Giants drown out the sound as long as possible.

Bill Corlett had been a captain for three years before the "Golden Age of Palaces" came to the river in 1860. He had been master of the *Eudora, Empire,* and *Urilda* in turn. Then he left the *Daniel Moore* by special request of its owner just as Captain John G. North began to build the *Chrysopolis*. Captain Jim Whitney and his charming bride, from New York, had suggested the boat to North, who was a partner in the California Steam Navigation Company. "You should have as beautiful a boat on your lovely river as any palace steaming on the Hudson," young Mrs. Whitney had said. North remarked, amiably enough, that when he had finished with the *Chrysopolis* even a Hudson river-palace would be a commonplace memory for a lovely lady.

North started off to the Mendocino forests with a group of workmen to select his timber. Bill Corlett, at loose ends for the moment, went with him. Bill didn't stay there long but he did get an enthusiastic sailor-man's idea about the kind of boat North was going to build. Corlett was back on the river long before the last of North's logs were felled in the Mendocino hills.

It was three months before North came back to San Francisco with his hand-picked trophies. Thousands of people packed the Mechanic's Fair Pavilion to see the logs stacked in a gigantic exhibition, long before they were struck by an adze. It took twelve horses to haul each log to the pavilion and, later, to the shipyard. As their tremendous lengths moved slowly through the city streets the crowd cheered for the *Chrysopolis,* which was to be the "most beautiful river steamer in all the world."

John North faced a dozen harassing problems. Heavy machinery had to be brought from New York during wartime scares and confusion. There were weeks of delay. Skilled boatbuilders were few and wages were high. Last of all, a real estate man named Dewey demanded $10,000 if the boat passed over two lots he owned which lay strategically between the shipyard and the water. North was forced to alter the launching course of his 1,000-ton hull to miss the Dewey property, a roundabout and expensive gesture. Mr. Dewey was much put out by such unfair and circuitous methods.

A regiment of decorators and painters was put to work. The quarter of a million dollar craft was painted white and gold inside and her fittings were best described as sumptuous. Her cabins held pictures by Thomas Hill, Charles C. Nahl, William Keith, Bierstadt, and Fortunata Arriola. Her cuisine could whet even a gourmet's taste and she shone with such a white glory and beauty of line as she lay beside the wharf before her first trip that an ecstatic poet praised her through twenty-four longish stanzas as "The Bride of the Golden River." Certainly she was the fastest and by far the most eye-arresting vessel on the river in 1860.

For years the *Chrysopolis* was the toast of the Sacramento. Her specialty was the "conveyance of bridal parties" and for ten years she was the fashionable "carrier of the elite." Her passengers liked speed and once she made a run from the capital city to the foot of Market Street in five hours and ten minutes, a record that stands to this moment. When she grew older and less sprightly they changed her name to the *Oakland* and rebuilt her in 1875 "from her hull up." Her lower deck was raised and she was lengthened. Then she began to shuttle back and forth between San Francisco and Oakland as a ferryboat. Thousands of transbay commuters rode her decks for thirty years without an inkling that they were standing over the keel of the oldest existing Sacramento River steamer.

But in Bill Corlett's time she was a splendid, flashing ship and even today old gentlemen with thumping canes speak of seeing her as she moved upstream on a moonlit night, her decks alight, and dance music drifting shoreward.

2

Away from the big steamers that Captain Bill Corlett knew, there was leisure on the Sacramento. Small fruit launches would start at dawn on the river and her tributaries, and run a zigzag course across the streams from ranch landing to ranch landing, the decks and holds filling at each stop with market-bound baskets and boxes of fruit and vegetables. All manner of river produce piled higher and higher until before the journey was half complete the boats themselves resembled drifting garden baskets.

Skippers and crews of the small boats knew the ranchers along the river by their first names and learned when they stopped whether Mrs. Smith was still ailing or whether Johnny or Clara had the mumps. The crews sang songs as they loaded the boats and the helpers on the bank joined in. It was a friendly, neighborly business, and few fruit launches rushed down the rivers ahead of schedule trying to pick up cargoes that were usually carried by someone else.

The *Chrysopolis* and *Antelope* were running to Sacramento and San Francisco on alternate days in 1860 when the *Defiance* carried the first calliope up the river, the air resounding with "The Girl I Left Behind Me," "You're All the World to Me," and a selected list of popular favorites. The *Defiance* was an opposition boat and had been refused a license to carry passengers on San Francisco Bay. But her captain had a plan to circumvent the "dastardly port officials." When he returned he loaded his passengers on barges near Collinsville and steamed on down to the wharf, calliope going and the barges swinging astern. The passengers sang and waved, while the port officials with deep-furrowed brows lined the wharf, fingering the latest port regulations. The opposition boats like the *Defiance* did their "tarnation best" to break the California Steam Navigation Company's "river control" and one company partner wondered orally if "the muckle-heads will ever learn their lesson."

Most of the river boats, for all their racing and snagging and boiler bursting, had good luck. Bill Corlett was always one of the lucky skippers. The upper river steamer *Fawn* burst her boiler without casualties in 1850, four miles above Sacramento City, and the *Martha Jane, Star,* and *Sacramento* were all snagged above the town. The *J. Bragdon* ran down the *Comanche* in '53 and sank her in Suisun Bay with a loss of ten lives. The *R. K. Page* blew up when racing the *Governor Dana* near Marysville and the *Belle* met the same fate in '56, killing her captain and a dozen of her crew. John Bidwell, who had a hand in the conquest of the state, was among the injured. The *J. A. McClelland* shattered her entire length into broken bits near Red Bluff, and the *Eureka* went down in Georgiana Slough. Yet there were only two great river disasters, separated in time, strangely enough, by a year, almost to the day. The vessels were two of the largest and most glittering packets of the company line.

The *Washoe* was built at Owen's Shipyards, on Hunter's Point, and her hull was a shapely marvel. Her new-type engines were perfect and only the boilers gave Captain Kidd anxious moments. They leaked on the first trip in 1864 and extensive repairs were made on them. These boilers had been constructed in Sacramento, and the flues in San Francisco. The faction in each city had different ideas about any imperfections found in the *Washoe's* equipment. Insinuations echoed back and forth about flues and boilers. Finally, a second mud-drum was installed under the boilers and the engineers guaranteed the equipment safe. The superstructure was repaired at the same time; it had recently been damaged when the tide had slapped the *Yosemite's* bow against the *Washoe* as she lay at dock.

Captain Kidd delayed the *Washoe* and her two hundred passengers at the Market Street wharf until 4 P.M. on Monday, September 5th. Kidd declared he would stay there until every other steamer had cast off. "No more foolish collisions for the *Washoe*," he said firmly. When the *Paul Pry* and *Antelope* were four miles up the bay and the *Yosemite* was eight minutes ahead, he finally gave the order to cast off. A reporter had interviewed him at three o'clock. Kidd had "pooh-poohed the idea of a race," remarking that he dared not get ahead if he could. "If something happened to check our speed," he pointed out, "we would stand a good chance of being run down by the *Chrysopolis*."

The *Antelope* landed at Benicia and fell behind the *Washoe*. The gleaming *Chrysopolis*, band playing in triumph, passed the *Washoe* below Rio Vista and Kidd asked the engine room for more speed. Chief Engineer Anderson gave it to him. But the *Chrysopolis* was out of sight as the *Washoe*, quivering in every deck plank, surged along some five miles below Rio Vista near the mouth of Steamboat Slough. Kidd stepped up to the wheelhouse again, restive and voluble. Pilots Baldwin and Easton were wheeling the course. At one minute past nine o'clock there was an explosion aft. There the head of the boiler ripped the decking as if it were thin kindling, hurling fire and shattered iron forward. Flames burst out in three places as the boat listed. Then screams and whimpers of agony took the place of the first great roar. Lights were out. Scalded people leaped into the river to die in cool waters. Some reached the bank and died, moaning, in the bushes; others ran until they found peace in some moonlit field.

Kidd and his officers, uninjured, rushed about doing their best at rescue work. Bob Morrison, first officer, had been asleep on the Texas deck when the blast threw him unscratched to the lower deck. An hour later Captain Foster and the *Antelope* found the wreck. A fisherman had come aboard with a sack of flour and a bottle of oil, and his hard hands were moving tenderly over burned bodies.

At dawn the next morning the *Antelope* reached the foot of R Street in Sacramento, running aground there for four hours before she could be towed to her berth at K Street. Her decks held dead and screaming victims on every square foot and her passengers had given over their cabins to scores more and worked through a heartsick night to ease the tortured. The great fire bells of the city began to toll and all Sacramento hurried to the river. The news spread like flame over dry tule lands. Many feared for friends and relatives returning on the *Washoe*. Ten thousand white-faced watchers reached the levee in an hour. A hospital corps was organized. The Vernon House on J Street was turned into a hospital. Cots were requisitioned and litters and gentle hands carried pitiful bundles from the *Antelope* to the waiting doctors.

A hundred people lay dead. Chief Engineer Anderson, dying with a twisted grin on his face, protected his captain with tortured words that set little beads of sweat on his forehead. "Only a hundred–and twenty-five pounds—in the boilers—when she blew. Rotten iron!" he gasped loyally. "Rotten iron!"

When Captain Kidd went back on the *Chrysopolis* next day he reported the *Washoe* submerged as far as the saloon deck and her lower cabin entirely underwater. "If the hull isn't badly damaged we can save her," he prophesied later in San Francisco. "She's in excellent position to be raised." At his insistence the owners sent out a salvage crew immediately. Speed was still a good word so far as Kidd was concerned.

Three months later the *Washoe* was once more a riverboat, freshly painted and with a new engine in her hold. But superstition kept her passenger list short. Shrewd Captain Kidd asked for another berth and Bill Corlett popped up as her master for a time. Company or opposition, a good ship was all the same to Bill.

Next year the *Washoe's* sister ship, *Yosemite,* was leaving the Rio Vista wharf at 6 P. M. of an exceptionally fine October day, windless and clear. Captain Poole and Pilot Enos Fouret had paused on the hurricane deck a moment, looking out at the deck throng of three hundred passengers they were carrying upriver. Poole was particularly interested in a troupe of actors and musicians from Maguire's Opera House, en route to a Sacramento City engagement. As the *Yosemite* swung slowly out, Maguire's "low comedian," J. H. Myers, was dancing a gay step for some children who were doing their best to imitate him. William Sharon was watching them and so was Senator J. W. Haskin of Mono. Some fifty Chinese had been summarily herded below by Bill Creigh, ship's freight clerk, only ten minutes before.

Roly-poly Myers had just burst into the most innocent doggerel he knew when the world ended. All the upper cabin, pilothouse, and deck forward of the smoke-stack rose in flame and smoke and chaos. Bodies hurtled through the air. A hundred passengers died in that instant and half that number in the next hour. Myers and his laughing children went jigging into eternity. Senator Haskin was blown into the river and swam safely to the opposite shore with a little girl in his arms. William Sharon's big hat went into the river, leaving him standing unhurt. Every Chinese below decks died. The burning wreck heeled against the wharf and horri-fied shore crowds began their rescue work.

A man without a head had crashed against Poole's body on the hurricane deck and battered him to the lower deck. He came up unscratched, a stroke of luck usual among river skippers during disaster. Before the explosion he had $150 in his right hip pocket and a gold magic-cased watch in his right vest pocket. When he came down he had neither money nor watch. The only part of the timepiece he ever found was the small cir-cular rim which held the crystal; that showed up in the littered fragments of the ship's barbershop.

The wreck was towed to an anchorage off Potrero Point and California Steam Navigation Company offi-cials with five captains in port at the time, Bill Corlett among them, made an exhaustive study of the hulk. They found some parts of the boiler "as thin as a felt hat." A great to-do began about defective iron and poor construction. But it died swiftly. The company dis-liked to continue such bad publicity. They were just launching the *Pacific,* forty feet longer than the *Chrysopolis* and twenty feet wider. Superlatives to usher in the *Pacific* ruled out talk of the luckless *Washoe* and *Yosemite.* Later, the company rebuilt the *Yosemite* for another try at river service.

Bad luck or an obstacle meant little in California's days of gold and wheat. When the *Pacific* lay ready for launching in San Francisco not enough soft soap or grease was immediately available in town to oil the keelways. The builders at once purchased $700 worth of "prime toilet soap," the entire perfumed supply of a delighted druggist. They melted it, mixed in a limited amount of grease, and the *Pacific* rolled down the ways in the sweetest-smelling ceremony on record.

When the Central Pacific Railroad bought out the California Steam Navigation Company on April 1, 1869, riverfolk soon found that this was a fight to the finish. The opposition steamer men were ready to burst with a new cargo of grievances. Only guns of light caliber had been used previously in river wars. As soon as an opposition boat ran on the river thereafter the corporation line reduced the fare to ten or fifteen cents, sometimes to nothing at all. If they met a stubborn opposition the Central Pacific actually paid passengers to ride on their boats.

Among the opposition craft, the *Enterprise* made a surprisingly long fight for patronage. The *Chin-du-Wan,* owned and operated by the scrappy Captain Zimmerman, also made an attempt to offer independent river service. Occasionally in midstream the *Chin-du-Wan* would slide up dangerously close to a company steamer and slap water heavy with yellow slickens over her bow in passing. At one time the combative Captain

Zimmerman advertised: "Legislative relief being so tardy, the People's Regulator, the *Chin-du-Wan*, will resume her regular trips." The "favorite steamer *S. M. Whipple*" ran, too, as an independent carrier but was finally forced to withdraw like her sisterships. Bill Corlett skippered her for some months. There was not so much fight in him now, but his convictions were as belligerent as ever. That later gold dredgers were now scraping millions out of the river sands did not make him feel more kindly. He was beginning to talk about the good old days on the river, when a man did his talking after the fact. He died in his thirtieth year on the Sacramento, his piledriver fists folded in a final gesture of peace. They buried him near his river, for it had been his life.

The year Bill Corlett died the Central Pacific constructed the largest ferryboat in the world, the *Solano*, to carry trains across Carquinez Strait from Benicia to Port Costa. Her larger twin, the *Contra Costa*, was built later to aid her, but now a tall bridge has taken over the tasks of both. Today they lie dismantled on a muddy bay shore, only slightly interesting to youngsters who shy stray rocks at their bulks from the tide line.

The *Amador*, too, once had her day on the river. She was one of the three largest river craft ever built and the hydraulic debris sometimes stopped her in low water. Often she was forced to wait for hours until some smaller boat pulled her over a sand bar. Her calliope was one of the sweetest on the river and Abe Harcourt, who played it, was a gentle and tolerant musicmaker. He used to sit, eyes watching the shore, playing for long hours the tunes his fellow passengers loved the best. Death walked over the deck one day and touched him on the shoulder while he played. He didn't want to stop. His fingers kept on pressing the keys as he bent over his board and the echoes of his last song hung in the air as if they would never die. When the stars are dim and the river moody with remembrance under a hazy moon, Joe Carlin of the ranchlands tells me he still hears Abe Harcourt playing his tunes on a steamer that runs forever upriver and never down.

The monitors finally drove the *Amador,* with her early-type high wheelhouses and pilothouses, from the Sacramento. Then, powered not by a walking beam, but by a heavy piston and massive crank connected with her shaft, she came to the bay for a long span of service as a ferry. When better boats joined the ferry fleet the *Amador,* like Ishi the last living Yahi Indian, became a pensioner of the University of California. Her machinery was taken out and she was anchored on the east side of the Oakland Estuary. The university crews stored their shells on her lower deck and the upper deck, with its long benches, was visited by university students on warm evenings.

I remember as a boy, on weekdays when the boat was mostly deserted, going across the narrow gangplank that led to the deck. The custodian was an oldster who owned a dog named Hatch. Often I have seen his slow old hands cleaning the *Amador's* huge golden eagles in the central panels of her paddlehouses. They shone as brightly as they had when the boat was a great packet on the Golden River.

3

John Wilkes Booth had spoken his last lines in Ford's Theatre when Rocky Hunt and his four brothers were boys along the Sacramento. Rocky and his clan didn't know that they were sharing experiences common to boys of their time along every American stream, rivers that were helping to shape national thought and purpose and initiative. It was a simple and direct world that they knew. Riverboys were having fun growing up with America.

Rocky's father had given up carrying water and tedding new-mown hay in Vermont to come to California. He married Nancy Cotton and bought land at Freeport. There he grew wheat and raised his sons. He liked fast trotters and there is a legend around Freeport that Dennis Rockwell Hunt and his single bay were never passed on the county road. More often than not, a Hunt boy rode beside his sire and exulted as the other racers fell behind.

The Hunts' Freeport home, with its severe lines, company parlor, tantalizing kitchen odors, and speckless windows, was only a few yards from the Sacramento. Beyond the windows lay the river, Rocky Hunt's first great mystery. He loved the sun and the boats, the floods and the flood drift, the trees and the shadowed swiftness of the water.

But he liked high-water times best. When a man of six is daily growing in physical prowess, the dangerous days are the good ones. It was of slight concern to him that a murky dawn showed the cows stanchioned in the barn knee-deep in floodwaters that had risen overnight. It didn't matter even though the stock had to be hur-

ried to the distant foothills by the Hunt boys, bare-
footed, breeches rolled to hip, each splashing rescuer
showing a cold, blue, and almost bare behind. Fences
and bridges were hurled away and the golden fields
stood deep in water. For weeks the county road was a
rowboat highway and the levees would be patrolled day

and night by anxious men, armed with shovels and rifles,
fearful of new breaks. To riverboys this meant only
high-water times.

When the river ran high it bore tangled treasure
drift. The Hunt rowboat, with two oarsmen, a bow
lookout, and Rocky in the stern attending both rudder
and pike pole, made adventure profitable. There were
various tricks to the business. The canny mariners always
rowed upstream a half mile, close in along the bank,

where the current was moderate. Once there, the boat was run boldly into midstream, where the yellow slickens swept past. Every ounce of strength the oarsmen had was needed to hold the boat even with a given point on shore. The toilers, by pike pole and by hand, began to hoist dripping wood into the boat. Sometimes it came in solitary blocks studded with pebbles from some far-distant sluice box; sometimes in billets of pine or oak or willow or cottonwood. Even huge trees, uprooted by a mountain torrent hundreds of miles away, were dragged ashore. The richest catches of all were gigantic masses of pilings and beams, wrenched from some bridge or wharf by the rush of waters.

In the quick, sharp struggle to win such a prize, every second counted and each yard gained upstream was valuable. With every hand manipulating rope and spike to grip the big logs, the half mile they had rowed upstream was soon lost. Matching their skill and strength and luck against the current, they fought to beach both boat and logs on their own bank. Sometimes they could, but often a heavy drift proved far too formidable a freight for four boys and a rowboat. When drifts bobbed by the front door it meant that no wheat money was paid out for firewood, and that the Hunt boys could "work up" cords of driftwood for the open market.

Taking a boat over the banks of the flooded river, with a shotgun and Nellie, the greyhound, was another daring adventure. A course was set over flooded grain-fields, fences and all. At times they went as far as the distant Y Street level in Sacramento. Skunks and coons were fair game, even if cornered on unsubmerged tops of fence posts. Bits of levee or knobs of land were alive with jack rabbits, gophers, and highly indignant squirrels. Gopher snakes and blue racers could be found coiled here and there around the tilted posts and in treetops.

High water or not, there was always adventuring for Rocky and the others. The undrained Sacramento swamplands were fascinating. No boy can tire of watching zigzagging snipe or high-circling sand cranes, whizzing blue-winged teal, white swans, swift low-flying blackjacks or the more stately canvasbacks. Rocky never confused the calls of the "honker" or the gray goose or the brant. Nor did he ever shoot a "kildee" mistakenly for a Wilson snipe. Rocky knew what kind of curlew was good eating and no schoolbook pictures were needed to tell him the difference between the meadow mushroom and its deadly counterfeit. Beach's Lake and the Willow Slough and the far-famed "Pocket" were among his favorite haunts. There was wild hog hunting in the denser tule growths and "niggerheads"—the stiff, charred stumps left after tule fires.

A boy had to be big enough to carry a shotgun and handle it in all kinds of weather before a full life was possible on the river. The Hunt shotgun was a muzzle-loading weapon with a ramrod and percussion caps. The easiest shots always turned up while the hunters were busy reloading. But if the hammer was cocked before the flight had passed beyond range, the Hunts were likely to have duck for dinner.

When fields were green with young grain Rocky had to keep the wild geese at bay. The geese quickly detected an armed watchman and kept away from him. But they knew when the guardian had no gun and they paid no attention to him then. Because of this, Rocky rode up and down the fields for many hours on one of the family buggy horses, voice hoarse and arms flailing in a vain effort to keep the geese in the air.

The old buckeye that sent its branches far out over the river's edge near Freeport stood by the neighborhood swimming hole. Names and hearts and arrows were carved into its ancient trunk. Beside it was a taller sycamore whose lowest limb, parallel to the water's surface, made a magnificent springboard. Some yards farther down the stream were willow trees with wild grapevines climbing thickly upward and clinging to their very tops. Beyond the willows were oaks, one of which, a fallen giant, stretched out into the river. Circling this obstacle tested the strength and courage of the best swimmers.

This Buckeye Hole was a fishing ground where the whitefish were bony but the perch just right. They were cooked at once on willow wands over an open fire to "piece out" lunches taken by stealth from the home larder. The salmon and sturgeon were gamy catches, many of the strikes proving too powerful for a thin line.

There was a final test for a boy who swam by the buckeye tree: to swim the river, from shore to shore. Rocky made his bid as soon as his three older Hunt oracles could be persuaded that he was ready. With a rowboat beside him, he "dog-paddled" his way across until with a final effort he reached out and gripped the willows on the opposite bank! It was worth the struggle. Respect was always shown a man who had "swum from shore to shore."

The S. M. *Whipple* rolling up the river in one of her frequent races, the *Amador* in her wake, had become Rocky Hunt's favorite steamer. In more leisurely moments her calliope was a summons that heralded her coming long before she made the bend. The windmill tower on the levee gave a fine view to all early comers as the *Whipple* came up the stream. "Give us a tune!" from the tower always got a response. Even the brass band of the competing *Sacramento* was a poor thing compared to a good calliope. As the *Whipple* slowed down and swung close in to play a request tune, the cheers and waving on the windmill made that old structure quiver.

The freight vessels that crowded the water were of little interest to Rocky. Small steamers and their fruit baskets on the way to market sometimes found him attentive as they zigzagged by, but he had only a casual eye for the *San Joaquin No. 2* as she bumbled importantly past hauling a string of four or five huge wheat barges, heavy laden, toward the bay.

The Grangers' Picnic at Beach's Grove was an annual event intensely anticipated. For weeks Mr. Hunt would carefully bring that fast nag, Pat Hunt, into condition, readying him to "lay the dust" on all comers. Mrs. Hunt always prepared, among other things, a chicken pie wide and deep. There was also serious training for foot races by each Hunt athlete. These preliminary trials usually left the Hunts too exhausted to run any winning races on the Great Day but served to keep the holiday properly important.

The day was worth waiting for. There were ice cream, oranges, popcorn, balloons, canes, candy, games, home-grown clowns, and occasional firecrackers smuggled in by determined wrongdoers. There were brass bands "in top wind." Horse and foot races were spirited contests and it was rumored that wagers were actually made on the events. Nothing was missing, not even the tame bear who jumped through the hoop of fire or the Orator of the Day who spoke fittingly of "this most happy occasion that fosters our most glorious American traditions." And as the Hunts rode home, Father flushed with victory on the track, Mother mulling over a new quilt pattern Mrs. Greer had outlined, the boys stuffed and dazed into quietude, Rocky had one persistent thought in mind: next year's May Day picnic.

4

Rocky Hunt had a great deal of respect for Freeport as a place. Its distinction came largely from the Liberty Flagpole erected there during the Grant-Colfax presidential campaign. The pole was the leading landmark for the countryside and particularly significant in a boy's eyes. Three sections, each made from a selected fir tree, were spliced together and bound by two sets of iron rings. The pole towered 130 feet high and was so well joined and tapered that it looked like a single, polished forest giant set up to do sentry duty by the river.

The raising of the pole had been more than a community celebration. Visitors rode for miles to witness Freeport's "Pole Day." Added to the villagers and their friends was an interested and select audience of canine well-wishers in remarkably good voice, at times capable of drowning out the cheering during the ceremony. Six men, a yoke of oxen, a span of mules, and a block and tackle went to work with a will. Up went the pole without a hitch. When it finally stood upright and unsupported, the clamor was heard for miles about. It was a moment of triumph and, for a while, Freeport

hatbands were much too tight for Freeport heads. In
later days, when the pole needed painting or the rigging
for the flag demanded fixing, a "Skysel Jack" was
always to be found, not unaware that he was a hero to
the young.

The flagstaff stood at the intersection of the Freeport road and the lane leading to the Ferry Landing,
only a few feet from the fence surrounding the Hunt
home. It was the supreme testing ground for a good
right arm. When a boy could hoist a green apple or a
stone up to the "first rings" he was good. Only the
bigger Samsons could throw up to the "second rings."
And there was no record of anyone ever casting over
the dignified and ever alert red rooster who kept an
endless watch of wind and weather from the tip.

The rooster was made of thin sheet iron, triply
coated with red paint. The plumes of his tail caught
the slightest breeze and his sharp beak always pointed
to windward. He ruled the Freeport roost for years
from his point of vantage and his was the first and the
last word about wind along the river. Boys rambling
the river bends were never tired of scanning the horizon
for the rooster's perch. Sometimes it seemed to make
lightning changes in its position. But the hikers were
brave as long as the familiar bird was visible.

In addition to the flagpole, there were other momentous institutions in Rocky's village. Mr. Andrew J.
Bump combined in one moodily Olympian personage
the grocer, postmaster, and saloonkeeper. The bright
red whiskers of Andy Greer, master maker of boots and
shoes, were often as significant a beacon as the flagpole
rooster. Tom Kirtland, the smith, had a singing voice
as powerful as his leather bellows and he never lacked

the attention of the young. Jim Lee, the bachelor dandy, solved all problems of dress for the Freeport folk. "Aunty" Eilbach ran the lone hostelry and Jim Lee was the only permanent boarder. She was definitely satisfied with this social cachet. The best-dressed man in Freeport lent tone to the place, Aunty always said.

Rocky was never in favor of certain attractions featured in Mr. Bump's general store. As well as being the distributor of candy "prize packages," the proprietor carried a small supply of dry goods and a large supply of wet goods, the latter proving far more profitable. Most of the men who drove back and forth on the Freeport road were Bump's customers. It was humane to allow one's sweating horses to stand at the cool, conveniently arranged watering trough and drop in for a glass of cheer or a cigar. Few of the callers smoked cigars.

Mr. Bump was also a devotee of games of chance although he never lost. The house always made a neat rake-off from each game in progress and sharp-eyed Bump dropped the take in a little velvet bag that he carried in a fat hip pocket.

Post office and candy counter were in the respectable end of the store, the front, just inside the broad plank porch that groaned under the weight of two benches dedicated to slumber and argument. Even when Andy Bump sold out to D. G. Webber, and Webber to Phil Riehl, there was war between the storekeeper and those who disapproved the "festering moral canker in our midst." It was impossible to do any fence straddling over such an issue in Freeport. You were either for the store or against it.

Directly across the street from the village "sink of

iniquity" stood Tom Kirtland's smithy. It was a cavern
full of fire and echo and song, of tongs and water
troughs, forges, iron tires, wagon wheels, leather bellows, horseshoes, iron rods, rivets, and boys. The back
part of the smithy was Jim Lee's carriage shop and
paint room. Jim was a genial and ingenious handy man,
never too busy to listen to youthful plans. There was
no barber in Freeport and Jim was usually called on
to cut a boy's hair when it became too shaggy. In high-
water times he made rowboats and once in a while he
did a special favor for some boy by making him a bow
out of a beautiful piece of hickory. He had a pate as
bald as a pumpkin and his beard was so thick that many
men swore they had seen a bird pop out of it in nesting-
time. Jim denied this, but his words lacked conviction.

Andy Greer, too, was a friend of the boys. His
cozy boot-and-shoe shop stood far enough away from
the store to be reputable and the shade of the huge silver
poplar above it was Andy's summer pride. He was full
of weird, bloodcurdling tales and strange little songs
about distant places and utterly worthless characters.
His regular seat was a piece of leather covering a hole
in a small bench and held in place by a circular row
of brass-headed tacks. The weight and motions of his
body had stretched the leather downward until it was
only an excuse for a seat and there he sat all day pegging
and sewing. Once in a great while Andy was good for
a little candy, but more often a chunk of his black
sewing wax was passed out to some friend as a signal
favor. He could work miracles by striking his keen
knife into a piece of waste leather laid on his cutting
board, drawing it in rapid circular motions until the

leather changed into a whiplash as a gift for the delighted boy watching him.

Mr. Greer was actually a sensitive and nervous soul, easily disturbed. When Rocky discovered that Andy was skittish, he engaged the Hunt clan in a scheme calculated to cause extreme perturbation and puzzlement to Freeport's bootmaker. A heavy weight, held by a wire, was arranged in the poplar's branches directly above Andy's shop. The wire was stretched deftly across the road and brought down along another tree trunk to the ground, where the Hunt rascals, hidden by brush, could control the weight without being seen.

One evening a great crash sounded horridly upon Mr. Greer's roof. Out popped an excited shoemaker. He looked up and around. No one about. No sign of miscreant or shooting star. The ground was solid and comforting. After a moment of perplexity he went in again, grumbling.

Another crash sounded immediately overhead. Out came Andy, hammer in hand. Still no one was to be seen, but Andy was unconvinced. There *was* mischief afoot. He rushed off to the store, came back with a lantern, and cautiously climbed upward. There he came upon the suspended weight!

With mounting indignation Andy traced the wire to the screen of brush. But the Hunt brothers were long since at home and innocently engaged as trenchermen around the Hunt table. Andy never found out who plopped that weight upon his roof. He never suspected the Hunts, who were such good boys anyway. It might, said Andy darkly, have been Frank or Ned Kirtland, or George or Ed or Charlie Greer, or "Doc" or Charlie Hack. Nor would Andy put it past those pests, Harry Beach, Ralph Towner, and Willie Green. Everybody but the Hunts was under suspicion for months.

5

The Freeport ferryboat had its landing on Hunt property and this gave the Hunts free passage at any time. It was considered quite the thing to ride back and forth when there was no other more promising diversion. Rocky once set a record of ten crossings in one day. The broad, flat-bottomed ferry was held in place by a big hemp rope and, later, by a wire cable made fast to an anchor in midriver, several hundred yards upstream, to which were attached a series of supporting buoys. The current forced the boat across the river, guided by the ferryman's windlass. To give the craft greater speed, a centerboard attached to its bottom caught the full force of the stream. A roped skiff always trailed alongside, ready to carry foot passengers across the river if travel was light.

Stant Myers, long of beard and short of patience, ruled the Freeport ferry. High-water times gave him anxious moments. Every year or so a fierce north wind or a raging current would tear the ferryboat loose and send it careening downstream. Then it was the devil's own job to coax the unwieldy boat back to a new cable at Freeport. Sometimes it took a whole day for the skiff and its rowers to make her fast to some tree on the levee. Then it sometimes took a week to walk her back upstream, using trees on the bank as posts and a stout rope stretched from them to the windlass.

Rocky was riding free one day on the wind-whipped ferry when the cable snapped. The suddenness of it made the roots of his hair tingle and put a small ghost of fear between his ears. Manuel Rose, who was minding the ferry for Stant Myers, gave a fine show of captainship. "Throw hoff the honker!" he cried. "Throw hoff the honker!"

It took the half dozen passengers a confused moment to execute Manuel's order. But they heaved the anchor overboard as soon as they were sure of his meaning. It hit the river with a heartening splash and only then did they realize that there was no rope attached to it!

Anchorless, the ferry sped on down the river. When, finally the boat was laboriously edged up the bank to her familiar berth, Stant Myers faced a very uncomfortable Portuguese. "I want that anchor," said Mr. Myers flatly. "Don't come back without it." For weeks thereafter a perspiring Manuel in a rowboat could be seen grappling the river bottom, unsuccessful but hopeful.

Rock Hunt, Sr., liked horses on a more competitive basis than "Old Man Hack," who spent hours breaking horses on the Freeport road, sitting like a "h'emperor" on the narrow seat of his ancient breaking cart, putting his two-year-olds through their paces. Father Hunt had a sportsman's eagerness for a good race. And he liked to win. He was never without trotting horses and Pat Hunt was a California champion of his time. Mr. Hunt had a liking for brushes along the country road, friendly tests of speed between neighbors that lent high lights to a workaday world.

One of his most persistent competitors was State Senator William Johnson. Dignity was the chief political tenet of Mr. Johnson and it was wise to address him pointedly as "senator." Gossip had it that not even his wife dared the intimacy of just plain Bill. He wore white gloves in every weather and he was never satisfied when his constituents betrayed the bad taste to pass his fast carriage span and light rig on the road. Only one of them made a habit of it, and the senator was continually promising himself to "ride Rock Hunt into the ground."

When Mr. Hunt, son Rocky in the seat beside him, met the senator and his gloves going in the same direction there was the usual warm greeting and the polite inquiries as to health and relatives, all custom-honored preliminaries, as the senator's fast-steppers tripped along beside Hunt's single bay. No acknowledgment or signal was needed to bring about a perfect understanding that a little brush was in the wind. Each driver put on his most guileless face with a fine pretense that a race between them was the last thing on his mind. As the conversation dallied over weather, crops, and the State Fair, little signs and pressures that could barely be noticed by an onlooker were urging the horses on!

Young Rocky, upright and eager-eyed, missed none of his sire's actions as the pace quickened. For a time the bay would be checked; then, with a gentle hint that they must be on their way, Pat Hunt would be given his head. The senator and his white gloves would fade into the rear as if they stood still, and Rocky Hunt's glee was never so restrained as his father's grin.

Change has come to Freeport and its river since Rocky Hunt was a boy. The old Hunt homestead and the scented garden are gone. The flagpole and the red rooster no longer stand as a landmark, and the sugar-pear tree, where the linnets vied with boys to capture the first ripening fruit, is no more. No buckeye tree sits by the bank, with initials carved deep in its trunk. The oaks are gone and the fallen giant of the drift. Even the bank is mutilated where some planners made a levee path for a railroad that went another way.

Out in the fields the mile race track where Pat Hunt reigned supreme is long gone. The thick patch of willows, a country for boyhood exploration, has met the woodsman's ax. Even the Upper Lake, fringed by acres of tall tules, scene of numberless floodtime hunts and summer fires, has been changed by the scientific drainage of a more exacting age.

And the boys of the seventies are scattered like the golden cottonwood leaves spun away by the river. Of the Hunts, Mark alone lives in the village. Rockwell Dennis Hunt—Rocky—is far south, dean of the Graduate School of the University of Southern California. But there will always be boys along the river. And the river will always have very much the same value to them even if life is different and even if it is affirmed, with vehemence, that no modern motorcar can hope to live long enough to approach the record of Peggy, the Hunt buggy horse, who lived long enough for four Hunt brothers to court their girls "with Peggy in front."

When old boys come back today, the river is still there, the flashing loveliness of it rolling by unchanged. Here is the only unalterable landmark of those returned from another century. Old, impossible fancies come down the breeze as fruit-tree cuttings are pungent in the air.

The rivers of America brought rhythm to a boy's world. That rhythm is never quite lost to boys grown older.

6

The men and women who have ridden up and down the river, singing and dancing and painting and writing and acting and making music, have brightened the life of the Sacramento. Some were famous when they came and some became famous because they came. Many made their way from other American rivers and states and some were entertainers from foreign lands. In the beginning, most of them were lured by California's gold and the reputed generosity of her new sons. After San Francisco they went upriver to Sacramento, thence to a "tour of the mines." Their coming was always heralded in advance, as much in the cities as in the "cow counties."

The years have brought new faces and new arts to the river but there is little change in California's greeting to the mummers and the music makers. Tibbett is as beloved as Genial John McCullough, and Helen Hayes as thunderously acclaimed as Kate Hayes, even if they have sung and played their way into our hearts in separate centuries.

At first the players used the river because it was the swiftest road. It was dustless and pleasant and one could relax for a few hours and feel its beauty before the hard if triumphant work in Sacramento's theaters and at the mines.

Mark Twain gave many lectures "at the mines" that brought ready laughter. Bret Harte and Joaquin Miller were less inclined to junkets of the sort. Edwin Booth, McCullough, Modjeska, Ristori, Edwin Adams, Ned Sothern, Lotta Crabtree, and Patti used the river-road. Charles Bishop, the great comedian, was the river's

SAN FRANCISCO BAY
IN 1853

darling and Ole Bull enslaved it with his violin. Charles C. Nahl and Thomas Hill and William Keith painted its life, even to the fat features of wealthy gentlemen who paid well. The show had gaiety and color and verve. Now famous players and singers still use the Sacramento to journey between the City by the Gate and California's capital. This long line of distinguished artists made their own history of the river, spending their talents on those who needed the lift of their sweet voices and songs and pictures and funny talk. They have added color and vigor to the theater and stature to American painting. They have freshened the tide of humor and folklore, and put the savory tang of western life into American literature.

Few of them ever ventured to the Upper River country, beyond Red Bluff. For most of them the river ended at Sacramento City and their itinerary thereafter led them into the foothills. An occasional theatrical troupe did ascend as far as Marysville, where Steve Massett of the *Herald* was writing California's first songs and where that tedious gentleman of letters, Dr. J. R. Poynter, was unaware that he was leading the physicians of the country into the writing field when he published the first novel in the state: "Entewa, The Mountain Bird. A Romance Founded On Facts. Marysville. 1852." But to the majority of entertainers and artists the Upper River was unknown territory.

They missed much. Of course, Joaquin Miller, that fabulous gadabout, reached the Upper River country in 1856, in ample time to write a stirring eyewitness account of the Battle of Castle Crags, fought in 1855. It is only incidental that Joaquin did not come to California until a year after the battle; certainly it

never bothered the chronicler of the conflict. His blood-
thirsty version still shivers California spines when he,
as "Mountain Joe's Boy," wounded, valiant, carrying
bullets in his mouth to have them handy, fought the
revolting Modocs, aided inconsequentially by volunteer
miners and friendly Shastans.

In 1855 the miners' tents sat like a great cloud of
feeding gulls along the path of the Upper River. Shovels
and "long toms" and pans threw tons of red silt into the
stream and the fish died in the poisonous flood. Indians
grew hungry and hatred of the white man prodded
them into open hostilities. They retreated, for the moment, into several citadel strongholds, one near dark
Castle Lake where dwelt their chief devil, Kukuparick.

Here the miners under R. P. Gibson, with their
Shastan allies, made a swift attack. Cries rang up and
down Castle Crags as the two parties met, Indian arrows against bullets. The guns won. "Mountain Joe's
Boy" went down with an arrow in his head and was
carried to a place of safety. Dorcas Dalla, the Modoc
chief, fell and on his dead body the Shastan chief,
Wielputus, danced until his bloody stage no longer gave
him footing. It was a great victory and Joaquin Miller
told its story with fine detail and gory emphasis. I am
sorry he did not see it. Some years later he did serve in a
volunteer though official United States Army company
which marched against some marauding Pit River
Indians. But the Battle of Castle Crags, which owes its
printed record to Miller's pen, was fought when he was
a dissatisfied boy in Oregon and not yet an actor in the
California scene.

The players of today have found a way to prove
that a river's work is never done. Only twenty years

ago some exploratory gentlemen pioneering a new art
discovered that the Sacramento was versatile. They
went back to Hollywood carrying a colossal idea. Since
then, as a result of their efforts, the river has played
a role in nearly every motion-picture theater on earth.
Many times you may have sat in suddenly tense darkness watching swift action on the screen: yellow pirates
battling over red decks on the Yangtze; steamboats
racing on the Mississippi, with boilers near to bursting;
a horse and rider daring death in an Ohio floodtide;
red men in canoes hunting scalps along the James; or
spike-booted he-men tossing logs and villains about in
technicolor abandon on the Columbia. You may not
have known it, but nine times in ten the Sacramento
was doubling for her sister rivers who received marquee
billing, the picturemakers having costumed her with
skill and adroitness for the cameras.

Previously producers had sent entire companies
around the world to shoot a river setting faithful to
the locale of their scenarios. This was before their explorers had examined the Sacramento. They found that
a trifling amount of background build-up along the
stream would duplicate any river scene on earth. This
realization fattened the producers' pocketbooks and
saved wear and tear on major stars occasionally forced
to take a 10,000-mile cruise to sometimes unhealthful
climates. More pictures could be made without a loss in
travel time. Location men with cameras rushed up and
down the river from Big Springs to Collinsville, making
shots to be filed, ready to be dragged out and critically
inspected when certain story demands arose. These
movie scouts never sleep and they have filmed the river
from every angle and in every mood, hoping that some-

day an unwritten story will need their records now sealed away in fireproof vaults.

If you remember *Steamboat Round the Bend*, *The Good Earth*, *Shanghai Bound*, *Huckleberry Finn*, *Of Human Hearts*, *The Adventures of Tom Sawyer*, *Devil's Cargo*, *The Pony Express*, and *Gold Is Where You Find It*, to mention only a few, you have seen the Sacramento in many of her various doubling roles.

When *The Good Earth* was made along the river scores of Chinese farmers in the vicinity turned to acting. It pleased them all very much and they never forgot it. When a later company arrived to make *Huckleberry Finn*, the Chinese moved en masse upon location. It took considerable patience and time to explain to the seasoned actors of *The Good Earth* that Mark Twain had omitted them from his novel. None of them appeared to have more than a vague idea as to who the author was. Finally, with great dignity, a spokesman talked up. "This Mark Twain," he said, "can't do this to us."

The director was adamant. He insisted he had no use for them in the cast. They abased themselves and offered to don burnt cork and appear as Negroes. The answer was still No. Then they sat down and refused to budge. In desperation the director hired them as laborers and went back to his megaphone. *The Good Earth* actors went to work, a trifle miffed at no camera attention, but sure of a pay check.

In *Steamboat Round the Bend* each of the quartette of steamers needed a little face lifting and architectural overhauling to present true Old Man River atmosphere. The various race shots were made less than ten miles upstream from Sacramento City and many an extra was a farm hand turned shore watcher or deck hand for a day.

Shanghai Bound was filmed on the Yolo side of the river. The Sacramento was draped as the Yangtze and technicians and artists recreated a Chinese village on its banks. The river steamer *San Jacinto* was rented for a month and her old friends had difficulty a week later in recognizing her as the none too-reputable *Hoi Ping,* a carrier in the Yangtze trade. Fifty tugboats and barges made fine supporting appearances, decked out as tousle-headed samples of Oriental river craft. And, again, many a farm hand played coolie for the cameras —at a distance.

No equipment or personnel were taken back to Hannibal, Missouri, when *The Adventures of Tom Sawyer* was filmed. Once more the Sacramento was drafted to play the Mississippi. The 70-foot steamer *Josie Lane,* which still navigates upstream as far as Tehama, was trepanned and deck-lifted and repainted to take the steamboat part in Mark Twain's story of American boyhood. Double dummy smokestacks were rigged to lend her the semblance of a last-century Mississippi smoke belcher and Hollywood smoke was supplied for the false stacks in moments of pulse-pounding action.

Gold Is Where You Find It, The Pony Express, and *Devil's Cargo* used the Sacramento and its historic background as a basis for their scenarios. In them the river had a chance to play herself and relive some of the spectacular moments that have been hers in the past. No doubt she will continue her career in pictures as long as they have need of her. She is one star who remains eternally lovely.

7

When men come to a new river and a new valley they bring their songs with them. The new land, in turn, gives them new songs out of the savor of life, and more folk history goes out across the American scene in ballads and endless verses that never grow less sweet or less important.

Our coming to California is still so recent that we are only now beginning to value the gifts of the folk singers above the work of their hands. Civilization came to California first from Spain, by way of Mexico. White men were interlopers on sufferance until the things gold could buy and new lands could promise brought the world to the Sacramento, the Great Valley, and the foothills. Those who came brought the world's songs and traditions, sung in a score of tongues, and they were not forgotten in the new state. Into the songs were written what men felt as they swung axes in tall forests and humped broad shoulders in the mines, as they herded cattle and sheep and hunted game along pine-crested slopes, as they fished and rode the river and its flashing tributaries, as they sowed and plowed and harvested fertile fields that once stood virgin as far as an Indian's eyes could scan the Penutian Empire.

But white men did not sing the first California songs. The red men did that, long ago. Some of their songs have been collected by the University of California and the Indian Bureau. Shaman-muttered incantations and chants were the closest approach the early Californians made to putting their history into words and music.

Spanish-California songs have come to us from

the pastoral era when gay señoritas tapped their heels
with the lightness of thistledown and saddle-scented
caballeros rolled their eyes and swaggered. Some of
them have been published by persistent seekers like
Eleanor Hague and Charles F. Lummis, or recorded on
records by others who, like Señora Luisa Vallejo
Emparán, last living child of General Vallejo, remember them out of the rich store of childhood's songs. Most
of them have the pleasing, pulse-tingling verve of old
Spain, bright and alive with castanets.

But there are songs being made along the river
today. A large group are inescapably merging with
more recent currents in folk and popular music, though
they may be as ancient in origin as King Harold who
died at Hastings upon the spears of Norman conquest.
Samuel Pepys, who made much of the ballad of "Barbara Allen's Cruelty," would strain puzzled ears today
if he could return and attempt to recognize the same
song, decked with new tones, and sung to a syncopated
guitar accompaniment. The words are little changed.
The only rewriting appears to be the fact that the lover
comes "from the Western states." Barbara still dies for
shame and he for sorrow and in death they sleep side
by side, a wholly satisfactory conclusion that ballad
singers have made no improvement on in more centuries than we know anything about.

Many of these songs come out of English tradition
and most of them are surely older than the British
colonial development of America. More recent Euro-
pean arrivals do not lack a pocketful of songs to add
to the wealth of their new homeland. If you have the
leisure and the inclination, you may hear along the river
and in the Great Valley songs that bright-eyed Serbs

chant in the heroic ballad form of their race. The men and women from Iceland sing the mighty Eddas with their sagas of men of valor and dragon-headed ships. In the river and valley towns one can occasionally hear strange songs of the Near and Middle East, some of them nearly as old as human history. Their melodies run from Syrian to Arabic, from Greek to Persian, from Turkish to Egyptian. There are lonely Spaniards who sing on far Sierra slopes, herders of sheep who make seasonal pilgrimages with their flocks from the delta islands and the valley to the hills. Added to their number has lately come a war-stressed tide of men and women and children from Galicia and the Asturias; bringing the traditions and songs and dances of a dying Spain where André Malraux has sung so hopelessly of man's hope. These Basques are proud, clannish folk, even in their extremity. To keep their hearts alive, they have brought their spirits of the open sky, Deburria, and Trufadeck, and the rest. They have seen the Lamminak, the fairy folk who say one thing and mean another, who lead travelers astray with smiling advice and change infants in their cradles so that a mother is often at her wit's end to know her own child. There is Aherbelste, skulker of the black heights, who pushes mountain wayfarers to their death; Tagus, deity of the beeches, who drops branches on careless heads during great winds; Laxarouu, of the high pasturelands, who has the power to enchant both sheep and human beings so that they never again may leave the hills. There is even Baïgorioc, who eats human flesh! All these have followed the Basques to their new home and I have been warned of them by my friend Jaime Olhaiby, who is well versed in these mysteries.

The Basques are as full of tales as old soldiers about chimney corners. Jaime Olhaiby tells of an enchanted princess living on the very top of Ping Pené in the Spanish Carlitte country, who was turned into a snake by a wicked fairy. The spell was not to be dissolved until a youth, pure in heart, had kissed her three times upon the lips. By chance there came a young man from the valleys and found the princess weeping into a flashing pool of frozen tears. He kissed her once because he pitied her. He kissed her again because, suddenly, she lay soft in his arms like a young girl in surrender. But he looked searchingly at her, being a very cautious young man, and saw that she was only a snake. He went swiftly away, with a hurried promise to return for a third kiss. War came and he forgot his princess. But with peace his thoughts turned to her again and once more he climbed Ping Pené, a song of conquest in his heart. She stood more beautiful than ever and he kissed her on the lips, again and again.

"And the princess was freed of the spell?" I asked courteously of Jaime.

"Of a certainty not," said he. "Nothing happened."

"But why?"

"He was a soldier," said Jaime sadly, "and he was no longer pure in heart."

So, I gather, the princess still waits atop Ping Pené, in the Carlitte country, for her deliverer. But Spain lies ravished below, and I feel that her wait may be long before a youth pure in heart can find time to scale the high place where she stands prisoned by evil enchantment.

It is difficult to say how many songs actually bear

the imprint of California, from "Dunsmuir to Marysville" to "Baby on the Stage Top." It is a fascinating
field for the folk explorer. Sidney Robertson has done
some excellent research in California and her friendly
journeys up and down the state have garnered a fine
array of folk songs and music for governmental records.
The task is an endless one of great variety, and those
of us privileged to linger awhile in the places where
the ballad singers foregather have never been bored
when the banjos and the guitars make music for words
that will live longer than books.

"Baby on the Stage Top" is doubtless Californian.
It was sung by drivers when their stages carried babies
in the fifties and sixties, doubtless designed to lull a
small squaller when the going was rough.

> Hush a by baby on the stage top;
>   When the whip cracks your cradle will rock.
> If the wheels fly off, the cradle will fall,
>   Down will come baby and cradle and all.

Californian, too, is the song called "By the River."
It carries in my memory a haunting cadence as I heard
it first by a small fire, in the river dusk. A straw-hatted
Oklahoma migrant sang it to a circle of his fellows,
plucking a guitar, his eyes shut as he sang:

> You were lovely long ago,
> With your rosy face aglow
>   By the river.

> It was true I loved you so,
> Ere the cruel war bade me go
>   From the river.

You were all a dream could be,
Sweetest maid a man could see
        By the river.

When I left, your eyes were sad—
I had always seen them glad
        By the river.

But the months ran fast away
As I fought the boys in gray,
        Beyond the river.

California's skies were blue
When I hurried back to you
        And the river.

But you slept beneath the land
With my ring upon your hand,
        Beside the river.

Here I linger at your feet
Where the river roses creep,
        Near the river.

Here I hold you in my heart
Where no man can make us part,
        By the river.

Another instant, the Oklahoman's eyes were wide
open and he was rolling out a song to plague his Kansas
friends:

Oh, they chew terbacker thin
An' it rolls down their chin
But they lick it up agin'—
        In Kansas.

Popular, also, are "Froggie Went A-Courtin',"
"Oh, Susanna," "Go Tell Aunt Nancy the Old Gray

Goose Is Dead," and fairly modern cowboy songs. Frequently heard is Bret Harte's "Flynn of Virginia," sung with all the dramatic skill of artists who know their business.

> Thar on the drift,
>   Back to the wall,
> He held the timbers,
>   Ready to fall.
> Thar in the darkness
>   I heard him call,
> Run for your life, Jake,
> Run for your wife's sake,
>   Don't wait for me!
>
> And that was all
>   Heard in the din,
> Heard of Tom Flynn,
>   Flynn of Virginia.

From the Ozark country come several songs describing the adventures of opportunists going west to the "last frontier." Not that the heroes start west in every one of these sagas. In one, at least, a wife talks her husband out of his journey by giving a stirring account of trail dangers to be encountered, Indians, gambling hells, and other carnal enticements. The oft-repeated refrain that the "stone that goes rolling will gather no moss" appears to be the final clincher in the long argument. A rather surprising number of melodies are given over to gamblers and their peccadilloes:

> Gamblin' Joe was a red-hot sport—
>   He drank his whisky with a snort.
> One day five aces dropped from his sleeve
>   Which same caused his poor old mother to grieve.

Many of the songs are highly suggestive, reflecting a generation of libidinous and cheerful sinners if the hero chances to be a gambler. The presentation of such songs is not unremunerative to modern troubadours. Many a foot-loose artist with a guitar sings his way from Shasta to Los Angeles, picked up along the highway by those who like music as they ride. "Better'n any radio concert," one of the singers informed me. "No bluenose ain't agoin' to cut me off the air!"

Every migrant camp, no matter how forlorn or sordid, has its quota of singers and guitars and mandolins and banjos. The balladeers know hundreds of songs, ditties of highwaymen with rubber necks who fear no rope, of Reno and Poker Flat and Nevada City gamblers, of risks attendant on the lives of lumbermen and miners and fishermen. The heroic legends of fist fights and fabulous feats of strength echo about campfires as long as men will listen, which is usually a considerable time since it is the boast of the troubadours that they can sing from dark to daylight without once "going back on their tracks." If men yawn, one of the singers will sweep into an especially racy and obscene offering to liven up the circle, possibly the ancient one about King John and the Bishop of Canterbury, as salacious as any that has lived down the years.

Logically enough, any great national event seems to distill a song out of the folk: Lindbergh's flight, Amelia Earhart's death, the building of the Golden Gate bridge, the sinking of the *Titanic,* or the Scopes trial. The famous sharecropper's lament has been adapted slightly by the singers to cover the depression and occasionally fits into an evening's sing in camp:

Try to raise peas, try to raise beans,
   All we can raise is turnip greens.
No use talkin', any man's beat
   With eleven-cent cotton and forty-cent meat.

Eleven-cent cotton and forty-cent meat!
   How in the world can a poor man eat?
Mules in the barn, no crop laid by,
   Grist mill empty and the crop goin' dry.

Well water low, nearly out of sight,
   Can't take a bath on Saturday night.
No use talkin', any man's beat,
   At eleven-cent cotton and forty-cent meat.

For only a short time have our folk songs and music been called significant, or anything beyond that profoundly irritating word "quaint." In our sometimes myopic American way we waited for word from Europe to assure us before granting that we were the inheritors of a folk art with an honest claim to beauty. There had been some misty investigations made by students of English literature who discovered colonial descendants of well-known English lyrics in the folk songs popular among the mountain dwellers of some of our southern states. But their conclusions never accomplished much. The mountain songs struck the ear peculiarly with their modal melodies and the casual researcher was quick to discard what he considered an artless product of no aesthetic worth.

A quarter of a century ago John Lomax published a collection of cowboy songs in which eight out of ten of the texts were printed naked and tuneless. No one even thought such a lack singular until Cecil Sharp,

the English musicologist, began noting down the tunes
and raising an ecstatic clamor over their excellence.
Then and only then did Americans begin to show interest in the superlative folk music so worthy of acclaim.
Men and women began making an effort to seek out
the melodies all around them, to record and preserve
their infinite variations. Today we recognize a dynamic
tradition echoing over every American river and valley
and hill where the people gather to keep their dreams
alive, to sing songs that have the tang and persistency
and quality of the American spirit. These songs record
a nation's mind without concealment or inhibition:
all man's fears and triumphs and catastrophes, all man's
lusts and high hopes and defeats. The songs are life as it
is, distilled out of the great hearts of little men, rhyth-
mic and uncensored.

8

The Upper Sacramento country has lost none of
its virginal beauty of forest and mountain and tumbling
river since Joaquin Miller wrote of it and Ben Parke
Avery traveled by "mud-wagon" from Sacramento
City to Sissons' in Strawberry Valley just under Shasta's
peak. But it is safeguarded beauty now. United States
rangers are vigilant on their high outposts, scanning the
horizon for the scourge of fire. They also wage a never-
ending scientific combat with microscopic tree pests
which threaten the forests with death. The Mount
Shasta Fish Hatchery, largest in the world, puts fifteen
million trout fingerlings into the streams each year, and
an added five million salmon. The wildlife is protected,
too, except in short hunting seasons. Wayfarers still

find the country as it was when the Penutian Empire ruled the Great Valley and the mountains.

The Sacramento rises from Big Springs, under Spring Hill, on the summer school grounds of Chico State College. Near by is bustling Mount Shasta City, immediately under the mountain. All its citizens talk about hiking and fishing and hunting and skiing and horseback riding. Dan Carlton, lean and friendly, has the entire pictorial history of lumbering in Siskiyou County for the past seventy years tacked up upon his office walls in the Mount Shasta City Garage, pictures that range from skid-row gangs to individual loggers about whom legends are still heard in American bunkhouses.

The whole section abounds in the unusual, the Oldest Inhabitant points out. Frank Bascom has photographed a huge "Sphinx Face" on Shasta itself, a towering example of nature's sculpture that makes the Egyptian original a locket miniature. On Castle Crags, nearly at the summit, stands an exact rock replica of an ape's head, complete to ears and eyes and hairline. Pumice Stone Mountain has a small crater that is nothing but a rose- and violet-hued morning-glory. There is an obsidian flow on Little Glass Mountain with a mud pot of hot lava still bubbling its dark brew, whistling a song as it works. I wish to warn the traveler against the Oldest Inhabitant, who guided me one day to a cavern where, he swore, a man could drop his hat into one opening and have it come sailing back through another, propelled by air currents far underground. I am still unconvinced, largely because I never saw my hat again.

The Oldest Inhabitant can also tell many yarns of the Lemurians, those strange people from stellar space who live in the inaccessible mountain fastnesses, inquired after by each carload of tourists who buy gasoline in the town and take their newspaper features seriously. The barrage of questions has become a little tiring to the townspeople but they bravely invent a new tale each time the curious arrive. It is good for business and it is not every town that boasts neighbors from space in its immediate back yard.

In the spectacular Castella region persists a legend of such downright authority that the visitor who doubts it had better keep his heresy to himself. In the early gold days, the story runs, a United States government pay train was ambushed by Indians while picking its tortuous way along the ridge near Castella. The pay train vanished and was never heard of again. But somewhere in the region, declares every native, the gold lies cached, hidden by the hostiles after the massacre and never disturbed since. It is an interesting anecdote and not too fanciful. Unfortunately, no United States government pay train ever wound its course with soldiers' gold along the Castella ridge. The entire story rises out of the imagination of an old-timer who got up one day with leisure on his hands and fabricated the yarn with golden trimmings.

Homes along the river now are not always swank modern houses or sixty-year-old white-painted mansions. There are houseboats along the stream, many of them inhabited only a few weeks a year by "city fellers," some of them the year-round homes of those who "follow the fruit" or set their hands to whatever odd jobs come along. If you are among those fortunates who know the river well you may recall a small houseboat cruiser with a green shamrock painted on its ancient side, poking laboriously along or lying tied up to convenient spots where owners are lenient about trespass. If so, you have seen Shanty Hogan's *Erin,* the "sweetest dam' boat on the river." Shanty is sixtyish, bald, thin, a bachelor, philosopher, wit, and an excellent judge of the lethal qualities of bad whisky. For a quarter century Shanty has chugged his way up and down the Sacramento and the San Joaquin, in good days and bad, sometimes lacking enough fuel for motor and stomach but seldom without a "drap of the best" to tide a man over bleak moments and give him a crisp and salty tongue for the condition of the country in general.

Shanty won the *Erin* in a raffle. She "sleeps me," as he puts it. The fact that she was originally named the *London* is conveniently forgotten by all those who knew Mr. Hogan before his affluent days as a leisurely yachtsman. Shanty is likely to become highly indignant and unpredictable if any injudicious reference is made to an English name in any remote connection with the *Erin.* It is as well to forget the whole matter if one wishes to be socially acceptable in the six-by-six cabin, open only to men of merit who win their way into the precincts because of deep sympathy with the Irish cause. A folding table, two stools, and a cot that moans when it is occupied are the principal furnishings. An Irish banner and various magazine pictures glorifying the undraped beauties of burlesque make a tasteful display on the restless walls. The two dingy windows cast a mellow glow upon all this. It has been my privilege to hear the story of Shanty's life, several times. It is unkind of me to note that it changes locale and action with each telling, except that our hero's birthplace remains adamantly in County Cork. But such discrepancies are of trifling importance. The biographical content is always diverting and the slight inaccuracies of an artist are of no moment.

I record sadly that I am no longer welcome aboard the *Erin*. I hasten to assure you that this unfortunate exclusion hinges entirely upon misunderstanding. Toward the end of one Hogan-flavored afternoon, with the most innocent of intentions, I suggested that Shanty change the name of his river-palace to *Eire*. After all, it seemed to me a gesture both fitting and seasonable. With a fine generosity I even offered to supply a vintage bottle for the christening.

An Irish hurricane rumbled out of Hogan's chest. I was driven forth with abuse and an utter lack of restraint. Any explanation for such a revolutionary change of name is still lost in the heat of parting. You see, Shanty takes his own time in catching up with current events and Erin is still Erin, so far as Shanty is concerned. Our quarrel may be patched up one day, when the news gets around.

Shanty occasionally tries his hand at trapping in the Delta regions, yet he can hardly be accepted as a fair representative of the modern trappers. Fur seekers may not be so numerous today as formerly but they are far from extinct. With his dogs and traps and light truck piled high with equipment, the trapper continues to make his way into the wilds of Modoc County and to other inaccessible spots where the almost uninhabited sections and their streams offer refuge to the weasel and the mink, the skunk, the coyote, and the fox. There is still a rich fur harvest for the persistent trapper.

Not long ago I met Sunset Sam Slade and Tim Geary on the outskirts of Redding, buying supplies

before trekking on to the Alturas country. Their four
dogs waited watchfully on a canvas-covered truck, not
quite at ease so close to civilization. Slade was enthusiastic about some traps. He hauled a few out for my
inspection. They were new-type chain traps.

"The old jaws are goin'," said Sunset Sam, with a
satisfied glint in his eye. "This business is finally goin'
scientific. This'll hold an animal without breakin' a
bone, crushin' 'em up, or hurtin' the pelt. An' you can
turn the females loose without hurtin' 'em."

Our talk ran to prospects and fur prices and fur
grading. The modern trapper is a keener businessman
than was his moccasined brother of the past. He knows
his markets and he keeps track of his price lists by radio.
No fur buyer can downgrade his pelts and keep his
business. He has been forced from the river up to the
source streams and he has the same regard for his free
life as had the mountaineers for theirs. But he has more
leisure for the movies, baseball, and the fleshpots than
the first fur men had for fandango and wassail. It is a
pleasant life and a man can keep in touch with the
world of sport and business and speed and madness by
radio as he works over the day's skins under the firelight
and the stars. At least that is Sunset Sam Slade's final
word in the matter. And he should know.

9

Probably the least-known sportsman's playground
in the West is part of the area of the Sacramento-San
Joaquin Delta. There the visitor still exults over a
gracious lack of billboards, gasoline pumps, and ham-
burger palaces. Missing, too, are the annual "Bass

Derby" days that enliven other river sections, where a man can win anything from a motorcar to a dog harness with a slight application of patience, luck, and sunburn lotion.

The inland islands there are threaded with waterways for fifteen hundred navigable miles, where yacht or cruiser or canoe or houseboat can find easy passage. This little-frequented section was once a cattail-covered swamp, stretching mysteriously for miles. It was known first to the native Penutians and later to pelt-stealing Michel La Framboise and his voyageurs. Today the territory is diked and dammed, given over to huge ranches set miles apart, with only a few firm roads crisscrossing here and there. The area is drained by a network of sloughs and these streams are the highways of the Delta.

The finest striped and black bass fishing in the world is found in these waters. Numberless, also, are perch, crappy, and catfish. Otter slides and beaver dams abound. Quail and doves thrive. At the end of summer come clouds of ducks and geese and snipe. Limitless and safe coverts give refuge to raccoon, rabbits, and opossum. Pheasants whir in the thickets and edible turtles take the sun with an unconcern bred of decades of comparative immunity. Boating in this wildlife land is a memorable experience. Light craft can nose for days through shallower channels where the animals have only hazy memories of men. You can fish or camp or hunt, or sit still if it pleases you.

The landmark of the region is Mt. Diablo, always a commanding guide by day as you wind along the shining streams. At night Diablo's airplane beacon flashes brilliantly in a tireless rhythm and it is comforting to the boat-camper in the Delta to see its red star on the distant heights.

Doubtless one day these watercourses will be crowded and no longer tranquil. I hope that day will be long delayed. For here is one singularly delightful region where a man's hours and thoughts are still in major portion his own and to which the vagrant time-waster and his tin-tossing, picnicking brood have not yet found the way. These streams are still a wilderness and he who knows the Delta can discover beauty and laughter and content within the sunlit reaches of an almost secret country.

I have seen the river from the sky, from Big Springs to its end beyond the Golden Gate. It runs through the land like a bright tree of life. Man has set a pattern on the vague distances and there is something unreal about the river and the valley, the mountains and the sea. But that is a vagueness being cleared from the air. Today airplanes drone back and forth in mathe-matically calculated zones over every inch of America, making a map of pictures. This master mosaic will soon be completed and, if you will, you can find in one of its numbered prints your own doorstep, the hill that played Vesuvius to your childhood, the unpaved road that steals upon your favorite trout stream, or check whether John Smith has sowed his acreage in a manner guaran-teed not to wrinkle the paternal brows in Washington.

The old river parade that the picture-map was too late to show is gone but it still engenders sentimental recollection. The little "variety stores" under steam that once carried everything from candy to kerosene for the river-bank farmers have vanished and the small fruit launches with them. The little ferries which crossed the river, using the current to propel them, always ready to drop their chains at the warning whistle of larger craft, are nearly forgotten. No throng rushes gaily to the landings begging a tune on the "steam piano" as the *Delta King* and *Delta Queen* plow their stately course today, carrying thousands of visitors from every land up and down the river.

This is not because the land does not produce. More than a million tons of crops are carried on the river each year. Sacramento City and Stockton are two of the great inland ports of the nation. The Sacramento leads all American streams, in both tonnage and value, in transporting products grown along her banks.

There has been much change in the river people and river homes. The tide of progress has made a pioneer way of life only a memory on the Sacramento and in the Great Valley. The virgin acres have been won. Now grandsons and great-grandsons, granddaughters and great-granddaughters, hold fast to the land their hardy forebears made fruitful. It is good to see so many of the old names clinging with amazing tenaciousness to the mailboxes along the river roads.

But the troubled world was not so close to river doorsteps last century. Now motorcar and radio and airplane and streamline propaganda have brought as much imaginative unrest to the Sacramento as they have to other American streams. All the modern mechanical laborsaving appliances are found in the river homes, and in the fields and orchards. Young people are no longer so eager to leave the river for the cities. Many enter the professions through the doors of Stanford and the University of California and a score of other universities and colleges. But more frequently now the agricultural colleges, at Davis and elsewhere, are tempering and turning out scientific young ranchers and farmers who know the problems of the soil and have as much delight in its fertility as their great-grandfathers had when first the green acres ran as wilderness before their eyes.

The great City by the Gate, where the Sacramento finds the sea, has retained its individual flavor while it discarded the windjammer for the China Clipper, the hansom for the motorcar, adobe walls for the skyscraper. Even the dullest perception cannot miss the uncommon pull and vigor of it.

This was the town that marched far out over the mud flats into the bay, with the steam-paddy biting down sandy hills, building wharves as it went, making room for tall walls and giving shipping a chance to tie up and unload its passengers and freight in the largest land-locked harbor in the world. It was the town of dueling; of organ-grinders and theaters that were never dark; of horses "dusting fast" on the Union Course and a dozen more ovals; of pitchmen selling cure-alls on every corner and of Yankee Jim and the Benicia Boy meeting all comers in smoke-filled prize rings; of the first "overland Butterfield Stage" before the coming of the rails. Here newsmen popularized dogs and cats and parrots and fire horses and mindless human beings; Norton I, Emperor of the United States, he of the gold braid, sword, and his own Imperial Currency; Topsy-Turvy, a witless old woman, who wore her clothes inside out; the Drummer Boy, who never ceased his noise; Uncle Freddy Coombs of giddy mayoralty aspirations; Bummer and Lazarus, two canine troublemakers; and others by the dozen.

It was the town of bear-and-bull fights; of "Mr. Shew's Daguerrean Saloon on Wheels"; of "Excursions" featuring every glittering military club from the Empire Guards to the San Francisco Blues; of wildcats and bull terriers in death grips on theater stages; of "Lottery Drawings," and of boys riding sleds down planked hill roads when it rained. It was the town where a city undertaker thought nothing of collecting top prices from the city for pauper burials by filling coffins with stones and stable dung. It was where crowds of gentlemen sporting glossy tiles sped in hacks from polling booth to polling booth, voting in each. Telegraph Hill was the only hill that traveled around the world; ships took its rocky sides as ballast and dumped them in their home harbors from Nagasaki to Sydney, from Apia to Buenos Aires. It is the town that but lately gave up its ferries for the largest suspension bridge on earth, towering out across the Golden Gate; and for the longest bridge in the world, that reaches from the waterfront by way of Yerba Buena to the Oakland shore. It is San Francisco.

American history began latest and ran fastest along the Sacramento. Other American rivers made and recorded their history with a certain order. But not the River of Gold. John Sutter's boat wake had scarcely died against the shore before a crashing human comber rolled over the river and his private empire. From the beginning, the whole Sacramento region was titanically quickened into life.

That tempo still exists on the river and in the valley. There is still about the pace of living a virility that will continue for a long time.

When men came here first they found a river and

a valley. Later, they wrote the final American chapter of the free soil, for they could go no farther. It was the only remaining continental land that an expanding young republic could take. When it was won, our last great wilderness became tilled earth, and the Pacific became America's fence line, the bright western border of the American dream.

Acknowledgment

A PLENTIFUL exactitude in days of the month and the southeast corner of places was only incidental in the plan that went into this book's making. I have been primarily interested in the folk of the river and the valley, the story of their sins and their hopes and their songs, the work of their hands and the shining things that walked out of their heads and their hearts. This, then, is the story of people, with a simple bit of chronological cord tied about chapters here and there where it was needed to bind the story more securely in your mind.

But in any such happy task of evaluation there is an indebtedness incurred to many historical source streams—to the river people of yesterday and today, to friends, to books, to newspapers, to ballad singers, to manuscripts, to grumpily hinged old trunks, to anecdotal gentlemen seated on fence posts. All these have been invaluable to me in writing this book.

The books I have read run all the way from Dr. A. L. Kroeber's *Handbook of the California Indian* to the countless county histories that deal so informatively of the river region. Numberless manuscripts have given me aid along the river trail, as have old newspapers and letters and those wholly admirable books of the *series* California. Most of these records have been consulted in Bancroft Library, of the University of California, and the California State Library in Sacramento. Dr. Herbert Eugene Bolton has been more than helpful in discussing certain phases of river life. A score more friends have given their time and interest and patience to suggesting material for the book: Mrs. Edna Martin Parratt, of Bancroft Library; Dr. George Tays, whose soon to be published book on General Vallejo afforded me added information on that pioneer figure; Miss Mabel R. Gillis and Miss Caroline Wenzel, of the California State Library; Frederick R. Soulé, of the United States Department of Agriculture; A. M. Barton, chief engineer of the California State Reclamation Board; Ad Schuster and Frank Kester, of the Oakland *Tribune;* V. S. McClatchy, of the California Joint Immigration Committee; Harry C. Peterson, curator of Sutter's Fort; Newell D. Chamberlain, of Midpines; William Ernest Rideout and Captain E. V. Rideout; George R. Conner, Orville Apperson, J. H. Schuler, and Dan Carlton, of Mount Shasta City; Mrs. Anne Bancroft Graham; Mrs. W. M. Vilas, of Red Bluff; J. J. Hill, of Berkeley; Elmer I. Jenks, of the Dunsmuir *News;* John G. Miller, of the Red Bluff *News and Times Sentinel;* R. B. Kercheval, of Sacramento; Edward A. Brown, of the California State Department of Industrial Relations; Hilmuth Ulmer, of Stockton; and Edmund G. Kinyon, of the Grass Valley *Morning Union.* The list is an endless one and I have doubtless forgotten others who should be named. Some of my notes have been made from a radio quarter hour by the University Explorer, from articles by Sidney Robertson and Dr. Paul S. Taylor, and from a thousand talks I have had along the river with those who live its life.

My story of a boy's life along the Sacramento is based on the unpublished memoirs of Dr. Rockwell Dennis Hunt, dean of the Graduate School of the University of Southern California, now a riverboy grown older.

JULIAN DANA
Piedmont, 1939.

Index

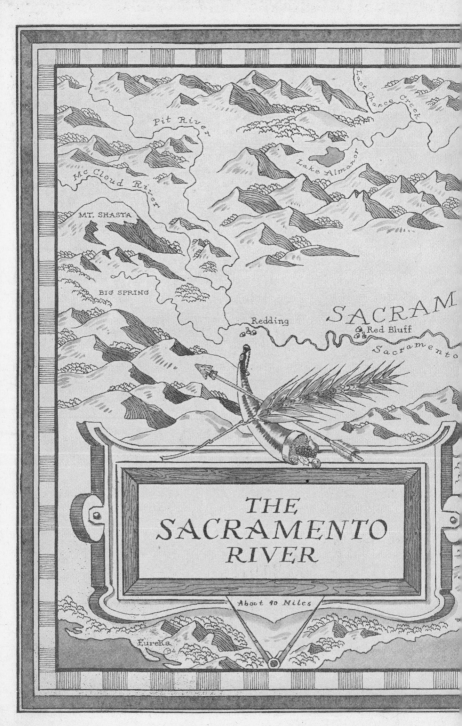

THE
SACRAMENTO
RIVER

About 40 Miles